MLflow in Practice

Definitive Reference for Developers and Engineers

Richard Johnson

Contents

6 Advanced Experimentation, Automation, and Pipeline Integration **135**

7 Security, Compliance, and Enterprise Readiness **161**

8 Observability, Monitoring, and Cost Optimization **189**

Introduction

In the rapidly evolving field of machine learning, managing the end-to-end lifecycle of models—from experimentation and development to deployment and governance—has become fundamental for success. This book, *MLflow in Practice*, provides a comprehensive and practical guide to MLflow, an open-source platform designed to streamline and standardize the management of machine learning workflows. It addresses the challenges faced by data scientists, engineers, and organizations in maintaining reproducibility, scalability, and operational rigor in their ML systems.

MLflow is structured around several key components, including experiment tracking, project packaging, model management, and a model registry. These elements together facilitate a robust MLOps environment that integrates with a wide ecosystem of tools and platforms. This text offers an in-depth exploration of MLflow's core concepts and technical architecture, detailing its deployment modes and interaction with established platforms such as Databricks, AzureML, Kubeflow, and Airflow. The book also covers critical aspects of security and access control, helping readers understand how to secure MLflow environments in enterprise contexts.

A significant portion of this volume focuses on advanced experiment tracking and metadata management. It delves into the MLflow Tracking API, providing practical insights into logging parameters, metrics, and artifacts for complex and distributed training scenarios. Strategies for custom logging and secure multi-user collaboration are extensively covered. Readers will also find guidance on designing scalable metadata storage solutions that support large-scale experimentation.

Packaging and reproducibility are central to reliable ML workflows. The chapters on MLflow Projects dissect project specification syntax, dependency management, and environment encapsulation using Conda, Docker, and virtual environments. Execution strategies across local, remote, and CI/CD platforms are analyzed to ensure reliability and automation in ML pipeline operations. The text also explains how to extend MLflow Projects with custom plugins and how to implement testing strategies to maintain reproducibility in production settings.

In addressing model lifecycle management, the book examines the MLflow Model flavors and pyfunc interface, along with artifact management and rigorous validation approaches. Techniques for exporting, importing, migrating, and serving models—including integration with scalable serving infrastructures such as Kubernetes and cloud services—are articulated with practical detail. The MLflow Model Registry section expands on governance, versioning, and lineage tracking workflows that support multi-team collaboration and regulatory compliance, including rollback and recovery procedures for maintaining lifecycle integrity.

Beyond the fundamental usage, this book extends into advanced experimentation, automation, and orchestration of ML pipelines. It outlines design principles for reproducible, modular workflows and their integration with orchestration frameworks and CI/CD systems. Approaches for continuous training, pipeline versioning, automated testing, monitoring, and hybrid cloud deployment scenarios are thoroughly examined.

Enterprise readiness and security are given dedicated attention, highlighting best practices in identity and access management, encryption, audit logging, and resilience architecture. Proactive vulnerability management and governance policy enforcement are discussed to prepare complex ML systems for production demands and regulatory environments.

Observability and cost optimization mechanisms are described in detail to empower operational teams with insights into system health, model performance, drift detection, and resource usage. Finally, the book presents real-world case studies from diverse sectors, illustrating the application of MLflow at scale, in regulated industries, edge environments, and research settings, offering valuable lessons and best practices.

Anticipating future trends, the concluding chapters explore emerging integrations and capabilities, including support for generative AI workflows, federated and multi-tenant architectures, collaborative distributed experimentation, and open interoperability standards. These perspectives position MLflow within the broader context of evolving MLOps ecosystems and innovation.

MLflow in Practice is intended as an essential resource for practitioners seeking to deepen their understanding and mastery of MLflow's capabilities. It is designed to equip readers with the knowledge necessary to implement, scale, and govern machine learning operations effectively within their organizations.

Chapter 1

MLflow Fundamentals and Architecture

Dive beneath the surface of MLflow to discover how its foundational concepts and technical architecture enable seamless, reproducible machine learning experimentation at scale. This chapter reveals why MLflow stands at the heart of the modern MLOps stack, guiding you through its inner workings, ecosystem integrations, and what sets it apart for both open-source enthusiasts and enterprise teams. Whether you're deploying locally or in the cloud, understanding these fundamentals prepares you for confident, informed adoption throughout the entire ML lifecycle.

1.1. Core Concepts of MLflow

MLflow is architected around four principal components: Tracking, Projects, Models, and Registry-each addressing distinct challenges inherent in the machine learning lifecycle. Collectively, they create an integrated ecosystem facilitating experiment management, reproducibility, model deployment, and artifact governance.

Understanding these components and their interrelations is fundamental for engineering robust ML workflows that scale from research experimentation to production deployment.

MLflow Tracking

MLflow Tracking is a comprehensive API and UI for logging and querying experiments. It addresses the complexity of managing multiple runs, hyperparameter configurations, code versions, and performance metrics typically scattered in disparate locations. The core abstraction is an *experiment*, a logical container for multiple *runs*, where each run records parameters, metrics, tags, and associated artifacts.

Runs are uniquely identified and can be organized hierarchically through experiments, enabling comparative analysis. Tracking's design promotes reproducibility by coupling each run with:

- **Parameters**: Input settings such as hyperparameters or configuration values.

- **Metrics**: Quantitative measurements like accuracy, loss, or throughput.

- **Artifacts**: Files produced during experiments, e.g., model binaries or visualizations.

- **Tags**: User-defined key-value metadata aiding in categorization and retrieval.

MLflow supports multiple storage backends (local file system, databases, cloud services), permitting flexible deployment architectures. The Tracking UI enables interactive exploration of runs, parameter sweeps, and direct comparison of metrics, accelerating iterative development and decision-making.

MLflow Projects

Reproducibility is a persistent challenge in ML pipelines due to environment variability and implicit dependencies. MLflow Projects solve this by encapsulating code in a standardized format that describes how to execute experiments in any environment.

An MLflow Project is defined by a repository containing an `MLproject` file specifying:

- **Entry points**: Named commands or scripts with arguments.

- **Environment specifications**: Dependencies via Conda or Docker environments.

- **Parameters**: Inputs for entry points with default values.

This structure enables repeatable runs regardless of underlying hardware or software, facilitating seamless collaboration and deployment. Project execution is automated through MLflow commands or APIs, orchestrating environment setup followed by script invocation, thereby minimizing manual configuration errors.

Moreover, Projects can integrate with Tracking to automatically log parameters and metrics from within the encapsulated code, ensuring continuity from experimentation through to reproducible execution.

MLflow Models

MLflow Models unify the packaging and deployment of machine learning artifacts. Model heterogeneity-ranging from traditional scikit-learn estimators to complex TensorFlow or PyTorch graphs-complicates deployment. MLflow Models abstract this diversity by defining a standardized model format for storage and consumption.

A model in MLflow comprises:

- **Model artifacts**: Serialized files containing learned parameters.

- **Spec files**: Metadata describing model type, environment, and input schema.

- **Flavors**: Language- or framework-specific interfaces (e.g., Python function, REST API, Spark UDF).

The notion of flavors enables flexible deployment pipelines where the same model artifact can be served via multiple frameworks or exported to different platforms. For instance, a single model may support local Python scoring, cloud-based REST inference, or batch scoring on Apache Spark clusters without reserialization.

MLflow provides simple APIs for saving and loading models, fostering interoperability and easing transitions from training to production.

MLflow Model Registry

Governance and lifecycle management of ML models pose challenges in maintaining quality, security, and traceability as models progress from development to production. The MLflow Model Registry introduces a centralized repository and workflow engine for model version control and stage transitions.

Key features of the Registry include:

- **Model versioning**: Immutable snapshots capturing code, parameters, and artifacts at discrete points.

- **Stages**: Defined lifecycle states such as None, Staging, Production, and Archived, controlling promotion and deprecation.

- **Annotations**: User comments, tags, and descriptions that enrich model metadata.

8

- **Access control and approval workflows**: Fine-grained permissions and review processes to ensure governance compliance.

The Registry tightly integrates with both Tracking and Models, linking experimental runs and packaged artifacts to model versions. This linkage enables holistic traceability from raw data acquisition, through experimentation, to production deployment and monitoring.

Interconnections and Workflow Integration

The four MLflow components coalesce to form a coherent machine learning lifecycle framework. Typical workflows involve:

- **Experimentation**: Using Tracking to log parameters, metrics, and artifacts generated by code encapsulated as Projects.

- **Reproducibility**: Leveraging Projects to rerun experiments consistently across environments, validating performance gains or bug fixes.

- **Packaging**: Saving trained models in standardized formats using MLflow Models, ensuring compatibility with deployment mechanisms.

- **Governance**: Registering models in the Model Registry to manage deployments, versioning, and approval workflows systematically.

This integration fosters a feedback loop where production models can be audited and iteratively refined through controlled experimentation, tracked comprehensively, and governed under enterprise-grade policies.

Seamless API interfaces bridge these components, with traceability preserved via unique run IDs, model URIs, and version tags. This architecture mitigates common pitfalls such as orphaned models, inconsistent environments, and undocumented experiments-empowering teams to innovate rapidly while maintaining operational rigor.

MLflow's core concepts provide a modular yet unified foundation for managing the complexity of modern machine learning pipelines. By abstracting experimentation, reproducibility, deployment, and governance into interoperable components, MLflow enables practitioners to build scalable, maintainable, and auditable ML systems across diverse organizational contexts.

1.2. MLflow as Part of the MLOps Ecosystem

MLflow has emerged as a critical component in the contemporary MLOps ecosystem, addressing a wide array of challenges inherent in managing the end-to-end machine learning lifecycle. By offering modular yet integrated functionality, MLflow facilitates experiment tracking, reproducible model packaging, and flexible deployment mechanisms. This positions MLflow uniquely at the intersection of data science experimentation, model governance, and operational scalability.

At its core, MLflow is designed around four primary modules: Tracking, Projects, Models, and Model Registry. The *Tracking* module serves as a universal API and UI to log parameters, code versions, metrics, and artifacts during model experimentation. This capability provides essential observability into the iterative ML development process, enabling teams to benchmark diverse algorithmic approaches and hyperparameter settings. The *Projects* module standardizes code packaging and execution environments, fostering reproducibility and portability across infrastructure. MLflow *Models* encapsulate trained models in a variety of deployment-ready formats, abstracting complexities related to target runtime environments. Finally, the *Model*

Registry introduces lifecycle management features such as versioning, stage transitions, and annotations, supporting robust governance frameworks aligned with enterprise compliance requirements.

When benchmarked against comprehensive platforms like Kubeflow and Amazon SageMaker, MLflow exhibits distinctive strengths rooted in its openness, modularity, and ease of integration. Kubeflow is primarily architected as a Kubernetes-native MLOps platform, emphasizing scalable pipeline orchestration, distributed training, and native infrastructure management. Its tightly coupled components, such as Pipelines, Katib for hyperparameter tuning, and KFServing for deployment, foster a holistic, albeit complex, environment that integrates deeply with container orchestration ecosystems. Amazon SageMaker offers a fully managed service encompassing all lifecycle phases, including built-in Jupyter notebooks, automated model tuning, managed endpoints, and monitoring. SageMaker simplifies cloud-native deployment but largely constrains users to the AWS ecosystem and its pricing models.

MLflow excels in scenarios where flexibility, hybrid cloud operation, and toolchain heterogeneity are paramount. Practitioners frequently adopt MLflow when existing infrastructure includes diverse orchestration platforms or when incremental additions to the ML lifecycle are required without comprehensive vendor lock-in. Its implementation-neutral design allows data scientists and engineers to maintain direct control over experimental workflows while benefiting from a centralized tracking and deployment framework. Thus, MLflow does not attempt to replace full-featured orchestrators but rather complements them by streamlining experimentation and model management layers.

Integrating MLflow into broader data and ML pipelines often involves harmonizing it with data versioning tools (e.g., DVC), workflow orchestrators (e.g., Apache Airflow, Prefect), and feature stores (e.g., Feast). MLflow's APIs enable seamless embedding within complex pipelines by exposing experiment metadata programmatically and facilitating automated promotion of models through lifecycle stages in the registry. This interoperability extends to monitoring and governance solutions, where MLflow serves as a source of truth for model lineage and performance metrics, ensuring traceability essential for compliance audits and risk mitigation.

A common pattern in production workflows is to employ MLflow for centralized experiment management and model versioning, while delegating pipeline execution to Kubernetes-based orchestrators or cloud-specific services. For instance, teams might use Kubeflow Pipelines for distributed data processing and training jobs, registering resulting artifacts and metadata into MLflow for unified visibility and subsequent promotion. Alternatively, hybrid architectures leverage MLflow's deployment flexibility, exporting models for serving in external platforms or containerizing MLflow models for scalable model serving infrastructures.

MLflow also addresses the challenges of scaling experimentation by supporting multi-user collaboration and remote tracking servers, facilitating reproducible research across organizational boundaries. Its support for multiple ML libraries and frameworks reduces cognitive load when integrating heterogeneous models, easing transitions from research notebooks to production-grade pipelines. Moreover, MLflow's extensible plugin system allows custom deployment targets and artifact repositories, aligning with complex organizational policies and multi-cloud strategies.

MLflow's pivotal role within the MLOps ecosystem derives from its capacity to unify disparate elements of experimentation, reproducibility, and model governance under a flexible and agnostic architecture. While Kubeflow and SageMaker offer comprehensive, opinionated solutions optimized for their respective environments, MLflow's strength lies in its modularity and interoperability, making it especially valuable for teams seeking tailored MLOps workflows that integrate smoothly with existing infrastructure. Understanding when to deploy MLflow-either as a standalone platform or in conjunction with orchestration and feature management tools-enables organizations to construct robust, scalable, and maintainable machine learning operations adapted to their technical and business contexts.

1.3. MLflow Architecture and Deployment Modes

MLflow is designed as a modular platform to streamline machine learning lifecycle management through well-defined client-server interactions, flexible storage backends, and multiple deployment patterns optimized for diverse operational contexts. Its architecture broadly consists of three core components: the MLflow Tracking Server, the MLflow Client, and the Storage Backend. These components collaborate to provide an end-to-end solution for experiment tracking, model versioning, and reproducible model packaging.

At the center of MLflow's architecture is the **Tracking Server**, which acts as the server-side API endpoint responsible for receiving and managing experiment data. It exposes RESTful APIs that enable interactions such as logging parameters, metrics, artifacts, and retrieving experiment metadata. The Tracking Server is stateless by design, delegating persistent data storage and retrieval to pluggable storage backends. This separation allows for scalability and extensibility in terms of persistence options.

The **MLflow Client** is a Python (or other language) library that provides the primary interface for machine learning practitioners to log experiments and query results. The client-side API communicates synchronously with the Tracking Server using HTTP requests. It transparently manages authentication, session handling, and data serialization for robust client-server communication. Because the client is lightweight, it can be embedded into diverse ML workflows with minimal friction.

One of the foundational architectural decisions in MLflow is its support for multiple **Storage Backend** types, each with its distinct role in managing experiment metadata, metrics, and artifacts:

- **Metadata Store**: Typically a relational database such as SQLite, MySQL, or PostgreSQL, which stores experiment metadata and metrics. This store ensures ACID-compliant updates and supports concurrency control, essential in multi-user environments.

- **Artifact Store**: A cloud/object storage (e.g., Amazon S3, Azure Blob Storage, Google Cloud Storage) or a local filesystem that holds large binary objects such as models, logs, and datasets. It is optimized for high-throughput streaming and retrieval rather than complex querying.

This bifurcation of storage concerns allows MLflow to scale horizontally by decoupling metadata from artifacts. Consequently, organizations can select storage services that conform to capacity, cost constraints, and regulatory needs.

Client-Server Interaction: The MLflow client initiates HTTP POST or GET requests to the server's REST API endpoints. For example, when an experiment run is started, the client sends a POST request to create a new run record; as the training progresses, parameters and metrics are logged with incremental POST requests. The server writes metadata into the SQL database, while artifacts are uploaded separately to the designated artifact store via signed URLs or direct file transfer protocols.

This design supports both synchronous and asynchronous client operations. In high-throughput scenarios, asynchronous logging of metrics allows improved responsiveness of the client without blocking the experiment pipeline. Moreover, all interactions are secured through TLS and, if configured, authentication tokens or OAuth2 credentials.

Deployment Modes are a defining feature for MLflow's adaptability across different infrastructure environments, each presenting trade-offs in operational complexity, scalability, and reliability:

- **Local Deployment**: MLflow can be run locally on a single machine, where the Tracking Server, metadata store (often SQLite), and artifacts all reside on local disk. This mode is suitable for individual development or small teams without extensive infrastructure. While simple, it lacks scalability due to limited concurrent access and provides minimal fault tolerance.

- **Managed Service Deployment**: Enterprises often deploy MLflow as a managed service within their data centers or private clouds. Here, the Tracking Server runs on dedicated servers or container orchestration platforms such as Kubernetes. The metadata store is replaced by reliable relational databases like PostgreSQL with replication enabled for high availability. Artifacts are stored on resilient network storage or object stores integrated inside organizational boundaries. Managed deployments enable centralized experiment management and fine-grained access control.

- **Cloud-Native Deployment**: Cloud platforms offer scalable, highly reliable hosting environments for MLflow. The Tracking Server can be containerized and deployed using cloud-native services like AWS Elastic Kubernetes Service (EKS), Google Kubernetes Engine (GKE), or Azure Kubernetes Service (AKS). Metadata storage employs managed RDS instances or cloud SQL databases, ensuring automatic backups and scaling. Artifact storage leverages cloud object

15

stores with regional redundancy. Cloud deployment leverages auto-scaling, integrated monitoring, and fault-tolerant
distributed storage, enabling MLflow to support large-scale,
multi-tenant environments.

Scalability considerations vary significantly across these
deployment modes. Local deployments handle a single user
and limited parallel runs; thus, metadata and artifact systems
have minimal throughput demands. In contrast, managed and
cloud-native deployments must accommodate concurrent access
from many users or automated pipelines, often requiring load
balancing of the Tracking Server and connection pools to the
metadata store. Artifact store performance becomes critical,
as large models and datasets necessitate high-throughput,
low-latency upload and download operations.

Reliability hinges on the choice of storage backends and deployment architecture. Local deployments offer minimal reliability
guarantees-if the host machine fails, data loss can occur. Managed
and cloud deployments implement redundancy via database replication, backup policies, and multi-zone object storage replication.
The stateless nature of the MLflow Tracking Server allows rolling
upgrades and container redeployments without loss of experiment
data, provided the storage backends are correctly configured.

MLflow's architecture emphasizes clean separation of concerns, resilience through stateless server design, and extensibility through
configurable storage backends. The choice of deployment mode-
from local development to cloud-native production-is driven by organizational scale, workload demands, and operational priorities
of scalability and reliability. This flexibility has been essential to
MLflow's broad adoption across heterogeneous environments in
real-world machine learning operations.

1.4. Interaction with Other ML and Data Engineering Tools

MLflow's design as an open-source platform for managing the machine learning lifecycle facilitates deep integration with a broad spectrum of ML and data engineering tools. Its modular architecture, consisting chiefly of Tracking, Projects, Models, and Registry components, enables seamless interoperability with various cloud services, orchestration frameworks, and data processing platforms. This section delineates the primary integration mechanisms between MLflow and major tools including Databricks, AzureML, Kubeflow, and Airflow, emphasizing practical strategies leveraged in production environments.

MLflow and Databricks

Databricks, the unified analytics platform built on Apache Spark, provides native and optimized support for MLflow. MLflow was initially developed within Databricks, resulting in a highly cohesive integration. Databricks users benefit from preconfigured MLflow Tracking Servers, automatic experiment logging, and a unified workspace for notebooks, jobs, and models.

The integration mechanism primarily leverages the MLflow SDK within Databricks notebooks. Experiment artifacts such as parameters, metrics, and models can be recorded with minimal configuration. Databricks' managed MLflow server provides scalability and security by abstracting storage and cluster management, including automatic support for artifact stores on AWS S3 or Azure Blob Storage.

Model deployment is accelerated by direct MLflow Model Registry support inside Databricks, facilitating seamless promotion of models across development stages. REST APIs exposed by Databricks enable integration with continuous integration and delivery (CI/CD) pipelines, further automating workflows. When combined with Databricks Jobs, MLflow functions as both a metadata layer and execution orchestrator, associating results and model artifacts with corresponding notebooks and clusters.

MLflow and Azure Machine Learning

Azure Machine Learning (AzureML) integrates with MLflow to address enterprise-grade ML lifecycle requirements on the Microsoft Azure cloud. This integration enriches MLflow's model management capabilities with Azure's cloud-native compute resources, experiment orchestration, and monitoring.

AzureML supports registering MLflow Tracking servers either by deploying on Azure Kubernetes Service (AKS) or using Azure Container Instances. The MLflow Tracking client can be configured to direct log requests to an Azure-hosted server. AzureML additionally introduces extensions to MLflow Projects to define environment dependencies using conda or Docker via AzureML's CLI and SDK.

Advanced integration typically leverages AzureML pipelines orchestrated via the AzureML SDK to execute MLflow-run projects and track corresponding experiment metadata. Using AzureML's compute clusters (e.g., Azure Machine Learning Compute or Databricks clusters) ensures scalable training execution, while MLflow captures detailed lifecycle metadata. Deployment workflows benefit from MLflow Models' compatibility with AzureML-managed endpoints, enabling easy promotion of models into production as web services.

Integration with Azure DevOps further automates the process, combining MLflow experiment tracking with Azure's source control and release pipelines, solidifying the continuous training and deployment cycle.

MLflow and Kubeflow

Kubeflow, an open-source Kubernetes-native platform targeting

18

ML workflows, integrates with MLflow through containerized pipeline components and artifact exchange mechanisms aligned with the Kubernetes ecosystem. This integration focuses on leveraging Kubernetes orchestration for scalable distributed training and reliable pipeline execution alongside sophisticated metadata management provided by MLflow.

Kubeflow Pipelines facilitate the embedding of MLflow Projects as pipeline steps. Through custom container images packaging the MLflow Project environment, Kubeflow executes these steps within isolated Kubernetes pods while MLflow aggregates run details centrally via its Tracking Server. This decoupling allows experimentation management independent of the underlying compute infrastructure.

MLflow's artifact store can leverage cloud-native object storage (e.g., AWS S3 or Google Cloud Storage) configured during Kubernetes deployment, ensuring persistent and scalable storage of experiment data. Kubeflow's metadata tracking component can be cross-integrated or co-used with MLflow's Tracking APIs, allowing visibility into pipeline execution results, model metrics, and parameters under a unified interface.

A successful strategy incorporates defining MLflow Projects that expose parameterized interfaces utilized as Kubeflow pipeline components. This modularity encourages experiment reproducibility, portability, and reusability across diverse Kubernetes environments.

MLflow and Apache Airflow

Apache Airflow serves as a widely adopted workflow orchestration engine in data engineering and ML pipelines. MLflow's integration with Airflow primarily revolves around embedding MLflow tracking and model packaging within Airflow Directed Acyclic Graphs (DAGs), facilitating orchestrated, repeatable, and monitored machine learning pipelines.

In practice, Airflow operators invoke MLflow Projects using the MLflow Python client or command-line interface, enabling the exact experiment configuration to be executed as pipeline tasks. Airflow's XCom mechanism shares MLflow run IDs, metrics, and artifact URIs between tasks, bridging discrete pipeline stages such as data preprocessing, model training, and evaluation.

MLflow Tracking Server can be deployed as a centralized service accessible by Airflow workers, enabling consistent recording and querying of experiment metadata. Airflow's scheduling capabilities complement MLflow by automating recurrent ML workflows, while MLflow adds granular experiment lineage and reproducibility through its model versioning and parameter tracking.

Combining Airflow with MLflow also ensures smooth integration into broader data engineering contexts, where ML training is tightly coupled with ETL, feature engineering, or data validation steps orchestrated by Airflow, thereby embedding robust ML lifecycle management into enterprise workflows.

Synthesis of Integration Strategies

A common thread across these integrations is the decoupling of ML experiment tracking and model management from the underlying compute and orchestration infrastructure. MLflow acts as a flexible metadata and artifact management layer, exposing standardized APIs and interfaces adopted by diverse platforms. Effective integration hinges on configuring MLflow Tracking Servers with artifact stores compatible with the target platform's storage systems and deploying MLflow Projects packaged in containerized or environment-specified formats.

In cloud environments such as Databricks and AzureML, native integrations streamline these configurations, reducing operational overhead. Conversely, Kubernetes-native platforms like Kubeflow demand explicit containerization and orchestration but benefit from MLflow's portability and standardized interfaces. Airflow complements MLflow by transforming ML experiments into scheduled, monitored, and chained workflows, integrating seamlessly into the data engineering ecosystem.

Ultimately, these integration strategies empower organizations to harness MLflow's lifecycle management capabilities in concert with sophisticated cloud-native and on-premises orchestration tools. This convergence facilitates reproducible experimentation, scalable training, and automated deployment while maintaining transparency and control over the end-to-end machine learning process.

1.5. Security and Access Control Overview

Securing MLflow deployments necessitates a comprehensive approach encompassing authentication, authorization, network security, and data protection. The objective is to safeguard the integrity and confidentiality of machine learning workflows, models, and metadata while maintaining operational accessibility for authorized users. The fundamental principles outlined here establish a baseline for securing MLflow instances in a production environment.

Authentication Models

Authentication is the first line of defense, verifying the identity of users and services accessing MLflow. MLflow itself does not provide built-in authentication mechanisms; hence, integration with external authentication systems is essential. Common models include:

- **Single Sign-On (SSO):** Utilizing identity providers (IdPs) such as LDAP, OAuth2, SAML, or OpenID Connect allows seamless user authentication across enterprise systems. This mechanism centralizes credential management and leverages existing organizational policies.

21

- **API Token-Based Authentication:** MLflow REST API access should be protected by issuing secure tokens with well-defined scopes and expiration policies. These tokens mitigate risks associated with credential leakage compared to static username-password pairs.

- **Mutual TLS Authentication (mTLS):** Particularly relevant for service-to-service communication within distributed ML pipelines. mTLS ensures both client and server mutually authenticate using X.509 certificates, preventing unauthorized access at the transport layer.

The choice among these models depends on deployment scale, existing infrastructure, and regulatory requirements. Regardless of the method, enforce multi-factor authentication (MFA) wherever possible to significantly reduce account compromise risk.

Access Control Policies

Fine-grained access control is critical for limiting user and application privileges to the minimal necessary scope, thus implementing the principle of least privilege. MLflow configurations should support role-based access control (RBAC) or attribute-based access control (ABAC):

- **Role-Based Access Control:** Define roles such as `Data Scientist`, `ML Engineer`, `Administrator`, each with explicit permissions related to experiment creation, model registry access, artifact upload/download, and administrative functions.

- **Attribute-Based Access Control:** More dynamic policies can be enforced based on user attributes, resource classification, or environmental context (e.g., time-based access restrictions).

Implementations often necessitate an external authorization service or middleware to mediate access requests, as MLflow lacks native enforcement mechanisms. It is recommended to integrate with industry-standard policy engines (e.g., Open Policy Agent) or cloud-native IAM (Identity and Access Management) services.

Network Security Considerations

Securing network communication channels for MLflow components is imperative to prevent interception, tampering, and unauthorized access:

- **Transport Layer Security (TLS):** All communication with MLflow servers, including API calls and artifact transfers, must be encrypted using TLS. Self-signed certificates are acceptable for development but production environments require certificates issued by trusted Certificate Authorities (CAs).

- **Network Segmentation and Firewalls:** Deploy MLflow services within segmented virtual private clouds (VPCs) or subnets, restricting access through firewalls or security groups to authorized hosts and services only. Avoid exposing MLflow UI or APIs on public endpoints without adequate protection measures.

- **Load Balancers and Proxies:** When scaling MLflow behind load balancers or reverse proxies, enforce secure termination of TLS and validate client certificates if applicable. Use these components to implement additional security controls such as IP whitelisting and request rate limiting.

Data Protection and Auditing

MLflow manages sensitive artifacts and metadata critical to operational and regulatory compliance. Data protection measures include:

- **Encrypted Storage:** Enable encryption-at-rest for back-end artifact storage (e.g., cloud object stores like Amazon S3 with server-side encryption). Metadata databases should also leverage encrypted volumes or database-native encryption features.

- **Immutable Logs and Auditing:** Maintain tamper-proof audit logs that track user activities, experiment changes, access to models, and metadata modifications. Logs should be stored centrally and protected against unauthorized modification. This supports forensic analysis and compliance reporting.

- **Backup and Disaster Recovery:** Regularly back up metadata stores and artifact repositories. Verified restore procedures ensure resilience against accidental deletion or ransomware attacks.

Minimal Security Requirements and Recommended Practices

To establish a secure baseline for MLflow deployments, adhere to the following minimal requirements:

1. **Enforce Authentication:** Ensure all user and system interactions require authenticated identities.

2. **Implement Authorization Controls:** Restrict privileges through well-defined roles or policies.

3. **Use TLS Encryption:** Protect data in transit.

4. **Harden Network Access:** Limit inbound and outbound traffic via firewalls and network policies.

5. **Encrypt Data at Rest:** Protect artifact and metadata storage.

6. **Enable Audit Logging:** Maintain comprehensive, secure logs of operations.

7. **Adopt Security Monitoring:** Integrate intrusion detection and alerting relevant to MLflow activity.

Supplement these with continuous vulnerability assessments and integration of MLflow security posture into organizational compliance frameworks. Careful planning and proactive management of these facets mitigate risks associated with exposing ML infrastructure and ensure the trustworthiness of the machine learning lifecycle.

1.6. Open Source and Enterprise Editions

MLflow, a widely adopted platform for managing the machine learning lifecycle, provides distinct offerings tailored to varying organizational requirements: the open source edition and enterprise-grade editions. While both share a fundamental architecture aimed at experiment tracking, model packaging, and deployment, their divergence lies in feature sets, scalability, integration capabilities, and support structures designed to address different stages of enterprise readiness and operational complexity.

The open source edition of MLflow delivers the core functionalities necessary for managing experiments and models. It encompasses four primary components:

- **Tracking:** Enables logging and querying of experiment metadata and metrics, supporting reproducibility and iterative development cycles.

- **Projects:** Encapsulate code in a reusable, reproducible format.

- **Models:** Provide standard mechanisms to package algorithms in multiple formats compatible with diverse deployment environments.

- **Model Registry:** Offers a centralized repository for versioning models, facilitating lifecycle management from staging to production.

Despite this robust foundation, the open source version is primarily intended for individual data scientists or small teams requiring flexible, low-cost solutions without extensive enterprise constraints. It lacks features essential for large-scale adoption, such as granular access control, advanced security integrations, and seamless scalability across distributed teams.

Enterprise editions of MLflow extend the open source functionality to meet stringent organizational demands. A key differentiator is the inclusion of advanced security and governance capabilities. Enterprise customers benefit from integration with centralized identity providers via Single Sign-On (SSO), enabling role-based access controls (RBAC) and audit logging. These mechanisms are critical in regulated industries where compliance with data protection standards and traceability are non-negotiable. Additionally, the enterprise platform provides enhanced data security through encryption at rest and in transit, as well as more robust data integrity assurances within model registries and artifact stores.

Scalability and availability present another dimension of differentiation. The open source MLflow primarily operates on standalone or containerized single-node deployments, suitable for moderate workloads. Conversely, enterprise editions offer fully managed or orchestrated multi-node clusters, capable of handling many thousands of concurrent users and model executions. This is facilitated through integration with cloud-native infrastructure and Kubernetes, which enables automated scaling, high availability, and fault tolerance. Such features reduce operational overhead and increase reliability for production-critical ML workflows.

From a feature standpoint, enterprise offerings incorporate advanced collaboration tools designed for cross-functional teams. These include automated workflows for model promotion, approval systems, and configurable notifications to streamline deployment pipelines. Additionally, enterprise MLflow frequently integrates with other enterprise data platforms and MLOps tools, enabling smoother interoperability within the broader IT ecosystem. This integration extends to continuous integration/continuous deployment (CI/CD) frameworks, enabling automated retraining and deployment triggered by data or code updates.

The support models available further distinguish open source from enterprise offerings. Open source users rely primarily on community-driven support channels, including forums, GitHub issues, and public documentation. While this provides flexibility and rapid innovation, it may not suffice for organizations requiring guaranteed service levels or rapid turnaround on critical issues. Enterprise editions are accompanied by dedicated technical support teams offering service-level agreements (SLAs), proactive monitoring, and bespoke deployment assistance. Such support reduces risk in mission-critical environments and accelerates troubleshooting and feature adoption.

When deciding between the open source and enterprise editions, organizations must weigh several criteria. The initial consideration is scale: smaller teams or research environments with limited compliance requirements may find the open source edition sufficient and cost-effective. As the number of users, models, and deployment complexity increase, the limitations of the open source offering in access control, security, and availability often become bottlenecks.

Regulatory and governance considerations strongly influence the choice. Organizations operating in sectors such as finance, healthcare, or governmental domains frequently require audit trails, secure credential management, and compliance with standards that only enterprise editions can confidently provide. Additionally, where operational risk must be minimized, enterprise support models and robust availability architectures justify the investment.

Integration requirements represent another pivotal factor. Enterprises leveraging diverse platforms for data processing, storage, and deployment benefit from the extended interoperability and automation native to the enterprise MLflow editions. Teams aiming to embed ML model operations within broader DevOps and data governance frameworks will find the enterprise tooling indispensable.

Finally, total cost of ownership (TCO) evaluation must consider not only licensing but also maintenance, support, and operational overhead. While the open source edition reduces upfront costs, larger deployments frequently require internal resources to replicate features natively present in enterprise solutions. This includes security hardening, scaling infrastructure, and achieving high availability.

MLflow's open source and enterprise editions serve distinct but complementary roles within the machine learning operational spectrum. The open source version underpins flexible experimentation and ML lifecycle management at modest scale, leveraging community-driven innovation. Enterprise editions layer on critical capabilities-security, scalability, governance, and professional support-to empower organizations to deploy ML at scale, with operational resilience and compliance assurance. Careful assessment of organizational size, compliance needs, integration complexity, and support expectations is essential to selecting the most appropriate edition for effective ML lifecycle orchestration.

Chapter 2

Experiment Tracking, Management, and Metadata

Go beyond simple experiment storage to master the art of managing, analyzing, and scaling machine learning experiments. This chapter offers a deep dive into MLflow's tracking system, revealing the techniques and infrastructure needed to ensure every run, metric, and artifact is captured, secure, and readily accessible. Unlock best practices and advanced strategies that transform chaotic experimentation into streamlined, auditable, and collaborative workflows.

2.1. MLflow Tracking API Deep Dive

The MLflow Tracking API is a versatile interface designed to record and organize machine learning experiments in a reproducible and scalable manner. Beyond fundamental logging of metrics and parameters, the Tracking API supports advanced features such as nested runs, custom tags, and extensible metadata, all of which facilitate granular and structured experiment management. These capabilities are essential for complex workflows requiring hierarchical experiment tracking and enriched descriptive context.

Nested runs provide the capability to organize related model training tasks within a parent-child relationship. By initiating a run inside another, researchers can capture distinct phases or modules of an experiment under a unified umbrella, maintaining the ability to analyze each component independently. This is particularly valuable when an experiment includes multiple submodels or iterative stages that need separate evaluation.

To create a nested run, the Tracking API's start_run function accepts a nested=True parameter. The parent run remains active while the nested run executes, and metrics and artifacts logged inside the nested context are scoped accordingly. This framework establishes a direct linkage in the backend store between parent and child runs.

```
import mlflow

with mlflow.start_run(run_name="Parent_Run") as parent_run:
    mlflow.log_param("param_parent", 5)

    with mlflow.start_run(run_name="Nested_Run", nested=True) as
    nested_run:
        mlflow.log_param("param_nested", 10)
        mlflow.log_metric("accuracy", 0.85)
```

In this example, Parent_Run encapsulates Nested_Run, allowing monitoring of aggregate and segmented outcomes. Nested runs are invaluable for capturing cascading experimentation processes such as hyperparameter searches, ensemble model training, or data transformation pipelines executed in discrete steps.

Tags in MLflow provide metadata annotations for runs that facilitate searchability, categorization, and auditability. While MLflow automatically logs certain standard tags (e.g., run ID, user), users can define custom tags to enrich metadata context. These tags can represent experiment conditions, environment identifiers, or any descriptive labels relevant to the domain or organizational conventions.

Custom tags are set using `mlflow.set_tag`, which accepts key-value string pairs. Tags are indexed and can be queried via MLflow's tracking UI or programmatic APIs, enabling comprehensive filtering and comparison across run collections.

```
import mlflow

with mlflow.start_run(run_name="Run_with_Tags") as run:
    mlflow.log_param("learning_rate", 0.01)
    mlflow.set_tag("dataset_version", "v2.1")
    mlflow.set_tag("team", "research")
    mlflow.set_tag("priority", "high")
```

This mechanism aids governance and collaboration by embedding contextual nuances such as data lineage, project phases, or deployment status directly into the run metadata. Consistent use of custom tagging can enhance traceability and search efficiency across large experiment repositories.

While parameters, metrics, and tags cover core experiment data, it is often necessary to log complex, structured, or lengthy metadata that falls outside these primitive types. MLflow Tracking API supports extensible logging through artifacts and serialized objects, thus enabling comprehensive experiment documentation.

Artifacts stored with runs can include configuration files, serialized models, images, or any custom files. These provide persistent storage alongside experiment tracking data, ensuring reproducibility and facilitating deep inspection of experiment artifacts. Artifact logging is crucial when experiments generate results that cannot be succinctly captured as simple metrics or tags.

```
import mlflow

config = {
    "layers": 4,
    "activation": "relu",
```

```
    "optimizer": "adam"
}

with open("model_config.json", "w") as f:
    import json
    json.dump(config, f)

with mlflow.start_run() as run:
    mlflow.log_artifact("model_config.json")
```

Furthermore, users can log arbitrary data formats by pre-processing and serializing metadata before logging as artifacts or use MLflow's log_dict and log_text for more direct structured logging. Combining these techniques delivers a flexible strategy capable of capturing detailed and heterogeneous experiment information.

The integration of nested runs, custom tags, and extensible metadata enables the construction of complex experiment hierarchies with rich descriptive context. This structure supports advanced workflows such as:

- Tracking parameter sweeps where each parameter combination corresponds to a nested run within a master experiment.

- Capturing model ensembles where individual base models are tracked as nested runs with respective metadata.

- Managing multi-stage pipelines where each step logs parameters, metrics, and artifacts distinctly but remains linked to the overall pipeline run.

In all cases, the hierarchical relationships are transparently maintained in the MLflow backend, allowing queries to traverse run families, filter by tags, and retrieve related artifacts efficiently. The ability to model experiment structure programmatically significantly improves reproducibility, debugging, and collaborative research.

Maximizing the utility of the MLflow Tracking API's advanced features requires disciplined metadata management:

- Define and document a controlled vocabulary for custom tags to ensure consistency across teams and projects.

- Use nested runs judiciously to avoid overly deep hierarchies that may complicate data retrieval and interpretation.

- Regularly archive or clean up artifacts to manage storage usage, particularly for large binary files.

- Leverage MLflow's query APIs and UI filters to monitor experiments continuously and extract insights from metadata relationships.

Such practices ensure the Tracking API remains an effective tool for scalable experiment lifecycle management rather than a repository of unstructured data.

MLflow's Tracking API provides a powerful foundation for capturing and organizing the complete context of machine learning experiments. Mastery of nested runs, custom tags, and extensible logging techniques empowers practitioners to build reproducible, navigable, and maintainable experiment hierarchies crucial for rigorous machine learning development.

2.2. Best Practices for Logging Parameters, Metrics, and Artifacts

Effective logging of parameters, metrics, and artifacts is fundamental to robust machine learning (ML) development workflows, particularly in scenarios involving distributed training, long-running jobs, and complex model architectures. The overarching goal of systematic logging is to ensure reproducibility, facilitate rigorous experimentation, and support comprehensive post hoc analysis.

This section delineates strategies and best practices that capture the subtle challenges and opportunities inherent to maintaining rich and meaningful experiment records.

Parameter Logging: Capturing Configuration with Precision

Logging parameters involves recording all relevant hyperparameters and configuration settings that influence model training and evaluation. A nuanced parameter logging strategy should consider the hierarchical and often conditional nature of configurations in complex ML pipelines. Parameters span a wide range, from global settings (e.g., learning rate, batch size, optimizer type) to more granular ones specific to components of the model or training environment (e.g., dropout rates in specific layers, regularization coefficients, data augmentation parameters).

To guarantee traceability and enable exact reproduction, it is advantageous to capture the full parameter set as a structured JSON or YAML object rather than logging disparate key-value pairs. This approach facilitates downstream parsing, comparison, and automated analysis pipelines. For distributed or long-running jobs, parameter logging should occur atomically at training initiation to avoid partial or inconsistent snapshots. When hyperparameter search algorithms or meta-learning frameworks dynamically adjust parameters during execution, changes must be logged incrementally with timestamps or training iterations to precisely reconstruct the evolution of parameter settings.

Metric Logging: Ensuring Granularity and Context

Metrics quantify model performance and training progress, serving as the primary feedback mechanism for tuning and comparing models. Unlike parameters, metrics are inherently time-series data, frequently computed at different granularities: per-batch, per-epoch, or at arbitrary checkpoint intervals. Capturing metrics with appropriate granularity depends on the experiment's objectives and the computational overhead that logging imposes.

Common practice involves logging a minimum set of core metrics (e.g., training loss, validation accuracy) at a frequency that balances insight against performance overhead. In distributed training across multiple nodes or GPUs, synchronization of metric logging is critical. Naive aggregation risks double-counting or losing granularity, so metrics should be aggregated at a designated master process or synchronized using reduction operations such as all-reduce. Additionally, logging confidence intervals or variance estimations alongside mean metrics can be insightful for understanding training stability.

For long-running jobs, it is important to store intermediate metric logs persistently and in a fault-tolerant manner, ensuring no data loss occurs due to system failures. Specialized time-series backends or experiment tracking tools that support incremental writes and resumable logging are recommended.

Artifact Logging: Preserving Models and Associated Data

Artifacts include any files produced during the training or evaluation process beyond simple numeric values: model weights, checkpoints, training logs, optimizer states, dataset snapshots, and generated outputs such as plots or tabular results.

Checkpointing is indispensable for long-running and distributed jobs where failures are possible, enabling recovery without loss of progress. Each stored checkpoint should be logged as a distinct artifact, annotated with metadata including epoch, metric values at saving time, and any relevant training context. Best practice includes maintaining a versioned artifact repository supporting retrieval by tags or unique identifiers, facilitating comparisons among checkpoints and models from different runs.

Complex model development often requires logging additional intermediate artifacts such as feature embeddings, attention maps, or calibration curves. These enrich interpretability and diagnostic capabilities but can lead to storage challenges. To manage this, selective logging policies should be articulated: for example, logging only the best-performing models based on validation metrics or archiving intermediate representations uniquely tied to analytical goals.

Strategies for Distributed and Long-Running Jobs

Distributed training introduces challenges in logging consistency, data volume, and synchronization. To address these, implement logging hierarchies that distinguish between local node logs and global aggregated views. Local logs record detailed information for debugging nodes, while aggregated logs summarize key aspects accessible for quick iteration.

Leveraging asynchronous logging methods prevents bottlenecks in training workflows, where logging calls dispatch data to a dedicated logger process or service, which then commits the information in batches. This architecture enhances training throughput while retaining logging fidelity.

For extremely long-running jobs, periodic checkpointing of both model state and logging metadata is critical. Systems should be designed to resume logging seamlessly post-interruption, appending to existing logs rather than overwriting.

Ensuring Meaningful Comparisons

To ensure differences in logged experiments reflect true variations in model or data factors rather than logging inconsistencies, adopt standardized schemas and logging frameworks. Consistent naming conventions and semantic versioning of parameters reduce ambiguity. When comparing metrics, leverage normalized forms and confidence bounds to avoid spurious conclusions from noise.

Experiment tracking platforms supporting tagging, grouping, and hierarchical metadata empower researchers to filter and compare experiments along multiple dimensions systematically. Building custom dashboards or visualizations that align with the logging schema further enhances the interpretability of logged data.

Illustrative Logging Pattern in Python

```python
import json
import time
from threading import Thread
from queue import Queue

class AsyncLogger:
    def __init__(self, log_path):
        self.log_queue = Queue()
        self.log_path = log_path
        self.thread = Thread(target=self._log_writer)
        self.thread.daemon = True
        self.thread.start()

    def log(self, record):
        self.log_queue.put(record)

    def _log_writer(self):
        with open(self.log_path, 'a') as f:
            while True:
                record = self.log_queue.get()
                if record is None:
                    break
                json_record = json.dumps(record)
                f.write(json_record + '\n')
                f.flush()
                self.log_queue.task_done()

# Usage example
logger = AsyncLogger('experiment_logs.json')

# Log parameters atomically before training start
params = {
    'learning_rate': 0.01,
    'batch_size': 64,
    'optimizer': 'Adam',
    'dropout_rate': 0.5
}
logger.log({'type': 'params', 'timestamp': time.time(), 'data':
    params})

# Log metrics incrementally during training, here just an example
    loop
for epoch in range(5):
    train_loss = 0.02 * (5 - epoch)  # dummy values
    val_accuracy = 0.8 + 0.04 * epoch
    logger.log({
        'type': 'metric',
```

```
        'timestamp': time.time(),
        'epoch': epoch,
        'train_loss': train_loss,
        'val_accuracy': val_accuracy
    })

# Signal logger shutdown
logger.log(None)
logger.thread.join()
```

{"type": "params", "timestamp": 1687400000.12345, "data": {"learning_rate": 0
.01, "batch_size": 64, "optimizer": "Adam", "dropout_rate": 0.5}}
{"type": "metric", "timestamp": 1687400600.54321, "epoch": 0, "train_loss": 0
.1, "val_accuracy": 0.8}
{"type": "metric", "timestamp": 1687401200.98765, "epoch": 1, "train_loss": 0
.08, "val_accuracy": 0.84}
...

This pattern illustrates asynchronous, structured logging capturing parameters and epoch metrics with timestamps, suitable for scalable and fault-tolerant pipelines.

Integrating these practices enables reproducible, transparent, and analytically rich ML experiments, empowering practitioners to address the challenges posed by modern, complex training regimes with confidence and rigor.

2.3. Custom Logging and Callbacks

In advanced machine learning workflows, static logging mechanisms frequently fall short of meeting the demands imposed by dynamic experimentation environments and diverse real-time requirements. Designing custom logging hooks and integrating event-driven callbacks facilitate more granular observability and responsiveness to external events and non-standard workflows. This section explores the principles for crafting such custom logging infrastructures, illustrates their implementation, and demonstrates practical scenarios where these extend experimentation capabilities substantially.

38

Fundamentally, logging within ML experimentation should be modular and decoupled from core algorithm execution, allowing asynchronous capture and processing of diagnostic and performance data. A custom logging hook typically functions as an observer pattern implementation: it registers with the training or evaluation loop and reacts when specific events occur, such as epoch completion, metric updates, or external triggers. These hooks are usually implemented as callable objects or classes with well-defined callback methods, registered through the experimentation framework's plugin system or direct function wrappers.

The design of a custom logging hook centers around three key activities: event registration, event handling, and output management. Event registration requires identifying discrete, meaningful moments in the workflow that generate actionable information. These can include dataset read completions, gradient norm calculations, hardware utilization updates, or the arrival of externally triggered events like manual intervention or integration pipeline signals. Event handling involves capturing the event context and selectively extracting or aggregating pertinent data. Output management must then transport, store, or visualize this information in a flexible manner, often leveraging asynchronous I/O or external monitoring tools for scalability.

Consider the following Python-inspired pseudocode snippet illustrating a minimal custom logging hook within a training loop framework:

```
class CustomLogger:
    def __init__(self, log_path):
        self.log_path = log_path
        with open(self.log_path, 'w') as f:
            f.write('epoch,loss,accuracy\n')

    def on_epoch_end(self, epoch, logs):
        with open(self.log_path, 'a') as f:
            f.write(f"{epoch},{logs['loss']},{logs['accuracy']}\n"
")

def train(model, data_loader, epochs, logger=None):
    for epoch in range(epochs):
```

```
loss, accuracy = model.train_one_epoch(data_loader)
if logger:
    logger.on_epoch_end(epoch, {'loss': loss, 'accuracy':
accuracy})
```

This example demonstrates how the CustomLogger opens a CSV file to record epoch-wise loss and accuracy statistics as incremental append operations. More sophisticated implementations might buffer data asynchronously or enrich logs with resource monitoring metrics.

Callbacks triggered by external asynchronous events require an additional layer of integration, often involving inter-process communication, message queues, or file system watchers. Machine learning workflows increasingly demand responsiveness to conditions such as user-initiated hyperparameter tuning, model checkpoint loading, or conditional early stopping criteria based on external signals. A callback designed to detect such events can be implemented as a listener thread or process communicating with the primary training routine via shared variables or event flags.

An example illustrating a callback reacting to an external "pause" signal file looks as follows:

```
import threading
import time
import os

class ExternalPauseCallback:
    def __init__(self, pause_file='pause.signal'):
        self.pause_file = pause_file
        self.paused = False
        self._stop = False
        self.thread = threading.Thread(target=self.
    _watch_pause_file)
        self.thread.start()

    def _watch_pause_file(self):
        while not self._stop:
            if os.path.exists(self.pause_file):
                self.paused = True
            else:
                self.paused = False
            time.sleep(1)
```

```
    def wait_if_paused(self):
        while self.paused:
            time.sleep(0.5)

    def stop(self):
        self._stop = True
        self.thread.join()

def train_with_external_pause(model, data_loader, epochs,
    callback=None):
    for epoch in range(epochs):
        if callback:
            callback.wait_if_paused()
        loss, accuracy = model.train_one_epoch(data_loader)
        print(f"Epoch {epoch}: Loss={loss} Accuracy={accuracy}")
    if callback:
        callback.stop()
```

Here, the ExternalPauseCallback continuously monitors for a file acting as a pause signal. When detected, it halts progress until the file is removed, enabling live intervention without terminating or restarting experiments. This approach scales to more complex signaling mechanisms such as REST API calls, message brokers (e.g., Kafka, RabbitMQ), or hardware interrupts, depending on deployment environments.

Flexibility in these event-driven designs supports automated experimentation pipelines with dynamic branching and conditional behavior. For instance, a custom callback might trigger additional data augmentation when validation accuracy stagnates or initiate model pruning at specific resource usage thresholds. Combining such callbacks with centralized experiment tracking systems, like MLflow or Weights & Biases, integrates reactive feedback loops that reduce manual overhead and improve model iterations' agility.

Real-world applications illustrate the benefits of these techniques clearly. At a major AI research facility, specialized logging hooks capture streaming GPU memory load alongside training metrics, enabling early detection of memory leaks and dynamic batch-size adjustment, preventing costly experiment failures. Similarly,

41

callback-based monitoring of external hyperparameter tuning services allows in-flight model parameter adjustments, fostering efficient distributed search and faster convergence.

Additionally, custom logging can enrich fault diagnosis by embedding debugging signals at multiple execution layers, from low-level device metrics to high-level algorithmic checkpoints. Hooks can be configured to record gradients, activation statistics, or error rates limited to anomalous conditions, minimizing performance overhead while maximizing insight. Such fine-grained logs also enable offline analysis and automated error localization models improving future runs' stability.

Custom logging hooks and event-driven callbacks provide indispensable tools for orchestrating complex ML workflows with enhanced adaptability and observability. By enabling interaction with arbitrary external signals and supporting rich data extraction during bounded execution phases, these mechanisms empower practitioners to build robust, automated experimentation systems aligned with evolving application constraints and operational environments.

2.4. Experiment Search, Comparison, and Visualization

Efficient retrieval, filtering, and comparison of experiment runs are critical processes in managing machine learning workflows, particularly as project complexity grows. MLflow provides robust interfaces—both a graphical user interface (UI) and programmatic search APIs—that facilitate navigating extensive experiment repositories. These capabilities enable practitioners to quickly identify relevant runs, understand metrics evolution, and derive actionable insights from iterative model development cycles.

The MLflow UI serves as a primary tool to explore experiment runs organized by experiments and experiments by projects. Accessing an experiment presents a tabular view summarizing each run's parameters, metrics, tags, and metadata. Runs can be sorted or filtered using built-in controls to narrow down candidates based on metric values, parameter combinations, or temporal constraints. The filtering syntax supports multiple conditions joined by logical operators, enabling queries such as retrieving all runs with validation accuracy above 0.85 executed after a specific date or those employing a particular hyperparameter setting.

For more complex or automated workflows, MLflow's search API allows programmatic access to the same filtering and querying capabilities found in the UI. The core of this capability centers on the function search_runs, which accepts an experiment ID or list of IDs, and a filter string expressed in MLflow's SQL-like syntax. For example, the following Python snippet retrieves runs with test error below a threshold and a specific optimizer:

```
from mlflow.tracking import MlflowClient

client = MlflowClient()
experiment_id = "123456789"
filter_string = "metrics.test_error < 0.05 AND params.optimizer =
    'adam'"

runs = client.search_runs(experiment_ids=[experiment_id],
    filter_string=filter_string)
```

The returned list of Run objects provides structured access to metrics, parameters, and tags, simplifying comparisons and further processing. Filtering through the search API permits integration into custom dashboards, automated reporting, or triggering downstream pipelines based on run results.

Comparison of multiple runs is enhanced by MLflow's ability to align and juxtapose metrics and parameters across runs. Differences in performance metrics are essential to judge the impact of algorithmic or hyperparameter modifications. MLflow UI supports selecting multiple runs and visualizes metrics in tabular and graphical forms, where trends and tradeoffs become apparent. For focusing on metric evolution over time or across iterations, line charts or scatter plots are available, highlighting how choices affect outcomes such as accuracy, loss, or inference latency.

Beyond UI capabilities, programmatic visualization can be realized by extracting relevant run data and employing libraries such as Matplotlib, Seaborn, or Plotly. For example, plotting accuracy versus training epoch for selected runs demonstrates convergence behavior and stability:

```python
import matplotlib.pyplot as plt

for run in runs:
    epochs = run.data.params['epochs']
    accuracy = run.data.metrics['accuracy']
    plt.plot(epochs, accuracy, label=f"Run {run.info.run_id}")

plt.xlabel('Epoch')
plt.ylabel('Accuracy')
plt.title('Model Accuracy over Epochs')
plt.legend()
plt.show()
```

An equally important dimension is visualizing lineage, which traces relationships among runs, models, and datasets. MLflow maintains metadata and tags that capture provenance details like the parent run, source code version, and data snapshot used. Visualizing this lineage helps understand dependencies, reproducibility, and impact of data drift or code changes on model performance. Integration with tools such as graph visualization enables representing lineage as directed acyclic graphs, elucidating the experiment workflow structure.

Experiment dashboards combining metrics trends, parameter variations, and lineage graphs amplify decision-making capabilities. Interactive filtering and drill-down features become essential in large-scale projects with thousands of runs, preventing information overload. Furthermore, embedding custom visualizations into MLflow's extension points or external platforms aids collaborative analysis across teams.

Overall, mastering MLflow's experiment search, comparison, and visualization frameworks streamlines the iterative machine learning cycle. By leveraging structured queries, comprehensive metric alignments, and intuitive visual representation of results and provenance, practitioners achieve the clarity and rigor necessary to optimize model development processes. These capabilities are fundamental in transitioning from ad hoc experimentation to systematic, reproducible machine learning engineering.

2.5. Security and Multi-user Tracking

MLflow, designed for large-scale machine learning experimentation, offers essential capabilities for securing experiment data while accommodating multi-user environments typical of enterprise deployments. Ensuring data confidentiality, access control, and comprehensive auditability is paramount in collaborative workflows, especially when teams operate within a shared infrastructure. This section addresses MLflow's core mechanisms for authentication, authorization, and auditing, focusing on how these features collectively support secure and isolated multi-tenant experiment management.

At the foundation, securing MLflow experiment data begins with enforcing robust authentication protocols. MLflow does not natively implement authentication but integrates seamlessly with existing Identity and Access Management (IAM) frameworks through its REST API and tracking server endpoints. By deploying MLflow Tracking Server behind an authentication proxy or as part of an infrastructure leveraging OAuth, LDAP, Kerberos, or cloud-native identity providers (e.g., AWS Cognito, Azure Active Directory), organizations can centralize user authentication. This prevents unauthorized access to sensitive model parameters, datasets, or proprietary experiment metadata.

Authorization complements authentication by restricting actions and experiment data visibility according to user roles and privileges. MLflow's design emphasizes experiment and run-level isolation by allowing users to define and manage experiment ownership and permissions externally. When integrated with policy enforcement points (PEPs) in service meshes or custom middleware, fine-grained access control can be realized. For example, a Role-Based Access Control (RBAC) system can ensure that only designated team members can create, modify, or delete runs within an experiment or access specific registered models. This is crucial for sustaining user isolation in multi-tenant environments, preventing data leakage across organizational boundaries or project silos.

To illustrate, consider a scenario where MLflow is deployed in a shared environment with multiple data science teams. Each team is provisioned an experiment namespace tied to their project credentials. Through middleware enforcing authorization policies, users can only initiate runs within their experiment spaces, with read-only access to shared baseline models. Such configuration supports secure parallel experimentation while preserving project data integrity.

Auditability is another critical aspect intrinsic to compliance and operational transparency. MLflow's tracking server logs metadata for every experiment, run, metric, parameter, and artifact interaction. These records form a detailed provenance chain, enabling traceability of who performed what action and when. However, out-of-the-box MLflow lacks an explicit audit trail user interface or immutable logs designed for forensic analysis. Enterprises often address this gap by coupling MLflow's event logs with external log aggregators and Security Information and Event Management (SIEM) systems like ELK Stack, Splunk, or AWS CloudTrail. This practice ensures that all user actions-experiment creation, parameter updates, model registration, and artifact uploads-are recorded and retained according to organizational governance standards.

Implementing immutable audit trails supports policies requiring

46

non-repudiation and facilitates regulatory audits in domains such as healthcare, finance, and telecommunications, where machine learning outputs have material impact. Leveraging MLflow's flexible backend store options, including SQL databases or object stores with versioning (e.g., Amazon S3 with bucket versioning enabled), further strengthens data resiliency and audit fidelity.

Isolation of user runs is enhanced through namespaces and experiment management strategies. Since MLflow experiments logically partition runs, assigning experiments to distinct projects or teams provides a structural boundary. Employing separate MLflow tracking servers or utilizing multi-tenant database schemas can isolate storage and querying layers, reducing cross-user interference and performance bottlenecks. Additionally, containerization and Kubernetes-based deployment profiles enable enforced runtime segmentation, ensuring that experiment execution occurs within isolated compute environments with appropriate resource quotas and security contexts.

A practical security workflow leveraging MLflow features may encompass the following components:

- **Authentication:** Integration with a corporate identity provider ensures user identity verification before accessing MLflow APIs or UI.

- **Authorization:** Middleware or service mesh enforces RBAC policies restricting experiment creation, run initiation, and model registry modifications per user roles.

- **Experiment Namespace Enforcement:** Experiment identifiers correspond to project or team boundaries, with database schemas or permissions aligned accordingly.

- **Audit Logging:** Real-time forwarding of MLflow server logs to centralized SIEM solutions creates a tamper-evident audit trail of all user activities.

- **Isolation of Compute Resources:** Kubernetes namespaces and pod security policies isolate experiment runs, preventing unauthorized cross-run interactions.

The MLflow model registry further extends security capabilities by assigning stage transitions and version management through access control. Teams can delegate model approval workflows to authorized reviewers, with all changes recorded as registry events. This controlled model lifecycle management protects against inadvertent deployment of unvalidated models and maintains alignment with organizational compliance.

MLflow's security and multi-user tracking functionalities rely on combining integrated authentication with externally managed authorization, experiment-level segregation, detailed audit logging, and orchestrated runtime isolation. This architecture facilitates collaborative experimentation across distributed teams without compromising confidentiality or governance. By embedding MLflow within a secured infrastructure stack and leveraging enterprise-grade identity services and logging, organizations establish a transparent, accountable, and resilient environment for managing machine learning workflows at scale.

2.6. Scalable Metadata Storage Backends

Robust metadata storage is critical for managing and operationalizing large-scale experiment data in advanced systems. The metadata repository must balance consistency, performance, scalability, and fault tolerance to support diverse workloads and access patterns. A spectrum of design options exists, ranging from traditional file systems oriented toward simplicity and local availability to complex, distributed SQL and NoSQL systems optimized for scale and availability. Understanding the considerations and architectural patterns guiding each choice is essential for selecting and implementing an appropriate storage backend.

48

At the most fundamental level, file systems-both local and networked-serve as the primary metadata storage for many smaller deployments. Their file-based semantics and ubiquitous support simplify deployment and reduce operational overhead. Metadata is typically persisted as structured files (e.g., JSON, YAML, or protobuf formats), allowing for straightforward versioning and incremental updates. However, file systems face inherent scalability challenges: concurrent access and atomic updates become difficult to guarantee under heavy, distributed workloads, making file systems unsuitable for large-scale environments where consistency and availability are paramount.

Transitioning to relational databases adds transactional consistency and indexing capabilities, which aid complex queries and metadata integrity. Traditional SQL backends like PostgreSQL or MySQL enable structured schemas for experiment metadata, supporting rich relational models that can enforce constraints and relationships. These systems excel when metadata has a well-defined schema and relational consistency requirements are strict. Moreover, mature ecosystem tools simplify backup, replication, and query optimization. However, scaling SQL databases horizontally remains challenging due to their reliance on strong ACID transactions and complex joins. As the volume of experiments and concurrent users increase, single-node or vertically scaled deployments become bottlenecks.

To address scalability and high availability, distributed SQL databases (e.g., Google Spanner, CockroachDB, YugabyteDB) extend traditional relational models with built-in replication and partitioning. They typically rely on consensus protocols such as Paxos or Raft to provide strong consistency across geographically distributed nodes. This allows metadata systems to maintain a globally consistent view despite network partitions or node failures, a critical feature for globally distributed experiments. These systems also support schema evolution and complex queries, making them suitable for sophisticated metadata schemas with strict consistency needs. Nevertheless, distributed SQL solutions introduce additional operational complexity and latency overhead, particularly for write-heavy or high-frequency metadata updates.

NoSQL storage solutions offer alternative design patterns optimized for scalability, availability, and schema flexibility. Document stores (e.g., MongoDB, Couchbase) provide schema-less metadata persistence, enabling agile schema evolution and flexible querying. Column-family stores (e.g., Cassandra, HBase) excel at handling wide, sparse datasets with high write throughput-characteristics common in large-scale experiment logs and telemetry metadata. Key-value stores (e.g., Redis, DynamoDB) emphasize ultra-low latency and high availability, suitable for caching or fast lookups of metadata. Many NoSQL systems employ eventual consistency models to maximize availability and partition tolerance per the CAP theorem, which necessitates careful application-level design to handle data reconciliation and conflict resolution.

Hybrid architectures often combine relational and NoSQL components to exploit their respective strengths. For instance, critical static metadata with complex relational dependencies can reside in distributed SQL, while voluminous, rapidly changing experiment logs and metrics are stored in a time-series database or column-family store. This separation enables optimized data models and query capabilities based on data access patterns. Metadata services can consolidate access via a unified API layer, abstracting the complexity beneath and offering consistent semantics to clients.

High availability and fault tolerance are crucial considerations for all metadata backends, especially when experiment results inform real-time decision-making pipelines. Replication, automated failover, and disaster recovery mechanisms must be integral to the metadata architecture. Database clusters employing consensus protocols offer strong durability guarantees against node failures. Backup strategies should include incremental snapshots and continuous archiving to minimize recovery windows. Monitoring and alerting help detect performance degradation or data anomalies early. Load balancing across nodes prevents hotspots and ensures smooth scaling during experiment bursts.

To operate metadata systems efficiently at scale, several best practices are advisable:

- **Schema design**: Model metadata schemas to minimize joins and complex transactions. Consider denormalization or materialized views for common query patterns to reduce latency.

- **Partitioning and sharding**: Distribute data across nodes based on experiment identifiers, timestamps, or logical namespaces to spread load and improve parallelism.

- **Consistency tuning**: Choose consistency levels (strong, eventual, causal) appropriate to metadata criticality and usage scenarios. For example, experiment configuration metadata requires strong consistency, whereas telemetry data may tolerate eventual consistency.

- **Caching**: Implement multi-tier caching layers to reduce backend load, employing write-through or write-back strategies to balance freshness and performance.

- **Monitoring and metrics**: Instrument metadata storage components for throughput, latency, error rates, and resource utilization. Employ anomaly detection for proactive maintenance.

- **Access control and auditing**: Enforce fine-grained access policies and maintain comprehensive audit logs to secure experiment metadata provenance.

- **Automation**: Automate schema migrations, backups, scaling operations, and failover to reduce manual errors and accelerate recovery.

The choice of metadata storage backend for large-scale experiment systems is driven by trade-offs among consistency, availability, scalability, and operational complexity. File systems provide simplicity but limited concurrency and durability. Traditional SQL databases add robustness and relational capabilities but struggle to scale horizontally. Distributed SQL platforms extend these features globally with strong consistency at the cost of complexity. NoSQL architectures offer schema flexibility and scalability with eventual consistency, necessitating application-level conflict resolution. Thoughtful hybrid solutions and adherence to proven design and operational patterns enable resilient, performant metadata storage infrastructures essential for supporting high-scale experimental workflows.

Chapter 3

MLflow Projects: Packaging and Reproducibility

Discover how MLflow Projects turns chaos into consistency by packaging your code, environments, and dependencies for flawless reproducibility. This chapter unpacks the essential building blocks and advanced patterns for structuring, sharing, and automating ML workflows, ensuring your experiments can be rerun and extended—across teams, platforms, and time. Whether optimizing collaboration or enforcing rigorous production standards, you'll gain strategies to bridge fast iteration with scientific rigor.

3.1. MLproject File Syntax and Semantics

An `MLproject` file—integral to MLflow project packaging—serves as the explicit specification of a project's configuration, orchestrating execution logic through clearly defined entry points, parameters, and runnable commands. Its declarative syntax, grounded in YAML, mandates disciplined organization to ensure reproducibility, clarity, and ease of collaboration across analytical workflows. Mastery of this file entails understanding both its structural components and the semantic constraints that govern their composition.

At the top level, the MLproject file begins with a schema that may specify name, conda_env (or docker_env), and a list of entry_points, the latter being the core executable targets within the project. Each entry point encapsulates a discrete operational mode, such as training, evaluation, or deployment, defined by a unique identifier and associated parameters. This modular design enhances composability and reuse, allowing the same project repository to encompass diverse workflows.

Entry points represent the named commands that drive the project, each described by a YAML dictionary with at least one executable directive, commonly command. This command is expressed as a shell-like string template supporting parameter interpolation via {{param_name}} syntax. Parameters may be optional or required and can possess default values, explicitly declared in an entry_points' parameters map.

A minimal entry point configuration looks as follows:

```
entry_points:
  train:
    parameters:
      epochs: {type: int, default: 10}
      learning_rate: {type: float, default: 0.01}
      command: "python train.py --epochs {{epochs}} --lr {{
      learning_rate}}"
```

Here, train defines the command line to run, parameterized by epochs and learning_rate. These parameters funnel user input to the command flexibly. Parameters support the basic scalar types—int, float, str, path—with type validation performed at runtime to preempt erroneous executions.

Defining parameters within entry points enhances configurability, with each parameter described via a dictionary containing:

- type: The expected data type; omitting this defaults to str.

- default: An optional default value used when no explicit value is provided.

Parameters augment clarity by enforcing typing and enabling self-documenting command interfaces. Their placement directly under parameters in each entry point scopes their availability solely to that entry. Cross-entry-point parameter reuse demands duplication or externalized configuration.

Example of a typed parameter without default:

```
evaluate:
  parameters:
    model_path: {type: path}
    command: "python evaluate.py --model {{model_path}}"
```

An attempt to invoke evaluate without specifying model_path results in runtime errors, signaling the required nature of the parameter.

The command field embodies the executable statement to invoke for the respective entry point. It typically represents a shell command with argument placeholders reflecting the entry parameters. These placeholders ({{param_name}}) perform a precise text substitution from supplied values, necessitating careful escaping and quoting to prevent injection or parsing issues.

A common best practice is to avoid complex shell constructs in command strings. Instead, define wrapper scripts or Python entry modules that parse parameters and handle environment preparation, thereby isolating complexity external to the MLproject syntax. This increases portability across shells and platforms.

Example 1: Modular Hyperparameter Sweeps

For iterative experimentation requiring hyperparameter sweeps, define multiple entry points with shared parameters but distinct commands:

```
entry_points:
  train_lr01:
    parameters:
      epochs: {type: int, default: 20}
      command: "python train.py --epochs {{epochs}} --lr 0.01"
  train_lr001:
    parameters:
      epochs: {type: int, default: 20}
      command: "python train.py --epochs {{epochs}} --lr 0.001"
```

While verbose, this explicitness avoids inline parameter logic, facilitating automatic discovery and invocation with minimal ad hoc scripting.

Example 2: Using Path Parameters for Data Inputs

Handling input datasets via parameters of type path ensures working directory consistency and MLflow tracking of artifacts:

```
entry_points:
  preprocess:
    parameters:
      input_file: {type: path}
      output_file: {type: path, default: "processed.csv"}
      command: "python preprocess.py --input {{input_file}} --
      output {{output_file}}"
```

Here, explicit path typing aids in validation and prevents accidental misuse of non-file values.

Common pitfalls and their remedies include:

- **Unquoted parameter substitutions:** Failure to quote substituted strings properly can result in command-line parsing errors, especially when parameters contain spaces or special characters. Enclose {{...}} expressions in quotes within the command string where appropriate.

- **Parameter type mismatches:** Omitting types or supplying incompatible values leads to failures at runtime. Declaring precise parameter types coupled with default values is essential for robustness.

- **Inconsistent parameter scope:** Sharing parameters across entry points improperly by name alone without duplication complicates workflow reproducibility. Use explicit parameters in each entry point or externalize shared configuration via environment variables or parameter files.

- **Complex shell logic in commands:** Embedding multi-step shell sequences or conditional logic in command strings hinders readability and portability. Delegate such complexity to auxiliary scripts invoked in a single command call.

A summary of best practices follows:

1. Declare all entry point parameters explicitly with types and defaults to ensure validation.

2. Use path parameters to manage data and artifact inputs or outputs.

3. Keep command strings simple and parameterized only via {{param_name}} substitutions.

4. Encapsulate complex logic in external scripts to maintain MLproject clarity.

5. Quote parameter expansions to avoid shell interpreter issues.

6. Design entry points as orthogonal, reusable units reflecting distinct project tasks.

By adhering to these conventions, MLproject files become not only machine-readable execution blueprints but also human-readable documentation that scales across collaborative teams and hetero-geneous environments. This level of rigor facilitates reproducibil-ity and maintainability, critical in advanced machine learning en-gineering contexts.

3.2. Dependency and Environment Management

Achieving consistency in software environments is critical for re-liable reproducibility, seamless collaboration, and robust deploy-ment across various stages of the software lifecycle. Variability arises from differences in dependency versions, system libraries, and configuration parameters, leading to the notorious "it works on my machine" problem. Effective dependency and environment management techniques are therefore indispensable for modern development workflows. Mastery of tools such as Conda, Docker, and Python virtual environments enables developers to construct portable and deterministic execution contexts, facilitating smooth transitions between development, testing, and production.

Conda is a cross-platform, language-agnostic package and environ-ment manager designed to handle complex dependency graphs, particularly for data science and scientific computing domains. It extends beyond pure Python environments by managing packages and binaries from multiple languages and system libraries, ensur-ing comprehensive environment capture.

A Conda environment is a self-contained directory that houses spe-cific versions of Python, packages, and dependencies isolated from the global installation. Environments can be created, activated, exported, and reconstructed with precise specification of package versions, platform compatibility, and channels.

The following command creates a new environment called env_proj with Python 3.10:

```
conda create -n env_proj python=3.10
conda activate env_proj
```

Package installation within the environment is straightforward:

```
conda install numpy=1.24 pandas matplotlib
```

To freeze the exact state of the environment, including channels and package versions, use the environment export command:

```
conda env export > environment.yml
```

The resulting environment.yml file includes all specifications needed to reproduce the environment on any system with Conda installed:

```
name: env_proj
channels:
  - defaults
dependencies:
  - python=3.10
  - numpy=1.24
  - pandas
  - matplotlib
```

Recreating the environment elsewhere is achieved by:

```
conda env create -f environment.yml
conda activate env_proj
```

Using Conda environments ensures that all dependency versions and their binary compatibility are captured precisely, eliminating discrepancies caused by mismatched libraries. The ability to switch environments quickly promotes rapid development and testing cycles without polluting the global package namespace.

Python's built-in venv module provides a lightweight mechanism to create isolated environments containing specific Python interpreters and packages installed via pip. While it does not manage system-level dependencies or non-Python binaries, it remains valuable for pure Python projects.

Environment creation proceeds as:

```
python3 -m venv myenv
source myenv/bin/activate   # On Unix/macOS
.\myenv\Scripts\activate    # On Windows
```

Dependency specifications are typically managed via a requirements.txt file, generated by freezing the currently installed packages:

```
pip freeze > requirements.txt
```

Installing dependencies from this file is then reproducible across environments:

```
pip install -r requirements.txt
```

Limitations arise from the absence of explicit system library management, so the approach is best suited for projects that avoid complex native dependencies or when combined with containerization.

Docker provides a complementary paradigm by encapsulating the entire runtime environment, including the operating system, system libraries, applications, and dependencies, into portable container images. Unlike Conda or virtual environments, Docker containers ensure identical execution environments regardless of the host machine's software landscape.

A typical Dockerfile defines a reproducible build:

```
FROM python:3.10-slim

WORKDIR /app
COPY requirements.txt ./
RUN pip install --no-cache-dir -r requirements.txt

COPY . .

CMD ["python", "main.py"]
```

Building the container image is performed with:

```
docker build -t myapp:1.0 .
```

Running the container executes the packaged application in an isolated space, avoiding conflicts with host system libraries:

```
docker run --rm myapp:1.0
```

Docker's layered filesystem allows incremental builds, accelerating development iterations. Moreover, container registries facilitate versioning and distribution of images, simplifying environment handoffs for deployment and scalability.

While Docker imposes a higher overhead in terms of resource consumption than Conda or venv, it guarantees maximal environment fidelity and is especially suited for microservices and production-grade deployments.

To eliminate environment-induced discrepancies across development, testing, and production, the following best practices are recommended:

- **Environment Specification Files:** Always maintain explicit dependency manifests (environment.yml, requirements.txt, or Dockerfiles) under version control. This allows rollback and auditing of environment changes.

- **Immutable Environments:** Avoid ad hoc installations outside formal environment management systems. Immutable, declarative environment definitions prevent "configuration drift."

- **Layered Approach:** Use lightweight virtual environments or Conda for development and testing, and Docker containers for production deployment where absolute reproducibility is paramount.

- **Continuous Integration Integration:** Automate environment reproduction and testing in CI pipelines to detect and resolve environment inconsistencies early.

- **Use of Hash Pinning:** Where possible, pin dependencies not only by version number but also by cryptographic

61

hashes to prevent supply-chain attacks and unseen package changes.

- **Cross-Platform Awareness:** When targeting multiple OS platforms, build and test environments explicitly for each target, leveraging multi-architecture Docker images or Conda's platform selectors.

Mastery of these techniques transforms environment management from a source of friction into an enabler of robust, collaborative, and scalable software engineering workflows. The choice among Conda, Python virtual environments, and Docker depends on project complexity, dependency characteristics, and deployment targets; often, a hybrid approach delivers optimal results.

3.3. Project Execution Engines: Local, Remote, CI/CD

MLflow Projects provide a flexible framework for packaging and executing machine learning workflows, accommodating a spectrum of execution environments that range from local development machines to remote clusters and fully automated CI/CD pipelines. Understanding these execution modalities is essential for scaling experiments, ensuring reproducibility, and integrating ML workloads into robust DevOps practices.

Local Execution

Local execution remains the foundational mode for running MLflow Projects. By invoking the MLflow CLI or API, data scientists and engineers can execute projects directly on their development machines, which facilitates rapid iteration and debugging.

The typical invocation uses the command:

```
mlflow run <project-uri> -P <param1>=<value1> -P <param2>=<value2
    >
```

In this context, `<project-uri>` can be a local directory or a remote Git repository. Parameters prefixed by `-P` pass inputs that control the project workflow. Local runs leverage the native environment, with dependencies resolved either through Conda environments specified in the `MLproject` file or through Docker containers if configured.

While local execution is convenient for proof-of-concept development, it is limited in scalability and does not inherently support distributed resource management. Thus, larger-scale projects generally require remote execution capabilities.

Remote Cluster Execution

To manage compute-intensive workflows and orchestrate multiple concurrent experiments, MLflow Projects can be executed on remote compute clusters or cloud platforms. This extends the project execution model by decoupling the actual runtime environment from the user's local workstation, enabling elastic scaling and resource abstraction.

Remote execution in MLflow predominantly occurs through integration with cluster management systems such as Kubernetes, Apache Spark, or cloud services (AWS Batch, Azure ML, Google AI Platform). The mechanism relies on the project specification layering a backend configuration detailing the cluster environment and authentication parameters.

For example, to execute a project on a Kubernetes cluster, one configures an MLflow-compatible run launcher specifying the cluster context and image repository. The metadata and artifacts are stored remotely, enabling reproducible runs and post-execution analysis.

The execution flow typically involves:

1. Submitting the MLflow project to the cluster via a CLI or API command.

2. The cluster scheduler provisioning compute nodes and initiating isolated containers or pods configured with the project environment.

3. Monitoring by the MLflow tracking server for execution states and capturing logs.

4. Gathering outputs and artifacts in a centralized artifact store like S3 or HDFS.

Remote execution allows organizations to enforce computational quotas, optimize hardware utilization, and run parallel hyperparameter searches. However, it demands careful orchestration to handle security credentials, network dependencies, and consistent environment replication.

Continuous Integration and Continuous Deployment (CI/CD) Integration

CI/CD pipelines bring automation and quality control to ML project lifecycles, enforcing best practices such as unit testing, reproducibility validation, and incremental delivery of models and services. Integrating MLflow Projects with existing CI/CD infrastructures-Jenkins, GitLab CI, CircleCI, or GitHub Actions-ensures that machine learning workloads conform to software engineering standards and operational constraints.

Automation can be introduced at multiple lifecycle stages:

- **Code Validation:** Automated linting and unit testing of data preprocessing and model code can trigger upon code commits or pull requests.

- **Environment Consistency:** Running `mlflow run` with predefined parameters ensures project dependencies and execution environments remain stable over commits.

- **Experiment Reproducibility:** Archiving MLflow run artifacts and parameters within the CI system guarantees traceability of model versions.

- **Model Promotion:** Successful execution and performance validation trigger deployment workflows, either registering models in a Model Registry or packaging them for production serving.

A representative GitHub Actions workflow snippet automating an MLflow Project run might resemble:

```
name: MLflow CI Pipeline

on: [push]

jobs:
  run-mlflow-project:
    runs-on: ubuntu-latest
    steps:
      - uses: actions/checkout@v2
      - name: Set up Python
        uses: actions/setup-python@v2
        with:
          python-version: 3.8
      - name: Install MLflow
        run: pip install mlflow
      - name: Run MLflow Project
        run: mlflow run . -P data_path=data/train.csv -P epochs
    =10
```

In more sophisticated setups, CI/CD pipelines orchestrate distributed experiments by triggering remote MLflow runs on cloud clusters, waiting for their completion, and aggregating results for automated validation and reporting.

Automation and Scalability Considerations

When scaling MLflow Projects in production-grade systems, several automation facets become central:

- **Parameter Sweeps and Experiment Management:** Systematically varying hyperparameters can be automated

65

via nested loops calling `mlflow run` or via integrated hyperparameter tuning utilities, enabling batch scheduling on remote clusters.

- **Artifact Versioning and Lineage:** Automated artifact storage linked to the MLflow Tracking Server ensures experiments' outputs remain auditable and reproducible across execution modes.

- **Environment Reproducibility:** Configurations for Conda/Docker environments must be rigorously maintained to replicate the same conditions across local and remote runs.

- **Security and Credential Management:** Remote executions involve managing cloud credentials, access tokens, and encryption methods within orchestrated workflows, which must be automated securely.

MLflow supports custom run configuration through scripted wrappers and launchers, enabling integration into complex DevOps chains. Organizations frequently extend MLflow with custom runners or orchestration platforms like Airflow or Kubeflow Pipelines for enhanced control and monitoring.

Ultimately, the choice among local, remote, or CI/CD execution engines depends on the project scale, resource availability, collaboration needs, and desired automation level. Mastery of these execution paradigms empowers data science teams to transition from ad-hoc experimentation to industrial-strength ML engineering and deployment.

3.4. Parameterization, Modularity, and Workflow Composition

Building robust machine learning (ML) pipelines for production demands an architecture that supports flexibility, scalability, and efficient experimentation. Central to achieving these goals are the principles of parameterization, modularity, and workflow composition. Together, they empower practitioners to structure complex workflows from reusable components, adapt executions through configurable parameters, and orchestrate seamless transitions across pipeline stages.

Parameterization: Enabling Configurable and Reproducible Executions

Parameterization abstracts the variability in pipeline execution by externalizing configuration details from the core logic of pipeline components. Instead of hard-coding dataset paths, hyperparameters, or environment-specific settings, these values are passed as parameters, which can be modified independently of code. This practice ensures that the same pipeline definition can accommodate multiple use cases-such as training different model architectures, altering data preprocessing steps, or switching between datasets-without altering the underlying implementation.

From an engineering standpoint, parameters serve as the primary interface between pipeline logic and environment context. A well-parameterized pipeline exposes critical options such as:

- Data sources and schema versions,

- Model hyperparameters (e.g., learning rate, number of epochs),

- Resource constraints or platform settings (e.g., batch size, number of workers),

- Feature selection choices or data augmentation techniques.

This design facilitates reproducibility by capturing parameters as part of the execution metadata, enabling regeneration of exact experimental conditions. Moreover, parameter sweeps and grid

67

searches become straightforward since parameter values are systematically varied without code changes.

Modularity: Building Blocks for Reusability and Maintainability

Modularity partitions the ML pipeline into discrete, self-contained components or stages that each perform a well-defined function. These modular units encapsulate responsibilities such as data ingestion, transformation, feature engineering, model training, evaluation, and deployment. The modular paradigm encourages separation of concerns, allowing teams to develop, debug, and optimize components independently.

Key attributes of effective modular components include:

- **Clear interfaces:** Inputs and outputs are explicitly defined, typically as well-specified data contracts or artifact types.

- **Idempotency:** Components produce consistent outputs for identical inputs and parameters, supporting cacheability.

- **Statelessness:** Avoidance of side effects ensures components can be reused in different pipeline contexts.

- **Configurability:** Each unit is parameterized for flexible invocation under diverse experimental settings.

Consider the example of a feature engineering module that normalizes datasets. By encapsulating normalization logic and parameters (e.g., scaling methods, feature subsets), different downstream pipelines-such as those targeting classification or regression-can reuse this component with varying configurations.

Workflow Composition: Orchestrating Complex Pipelines from Atomic Units

Workflow composition formalizes the method by which modular components are connected into directed acyclic graphs (DAGs) representing complete ML pipelines. Composition defines the data flow and execution order, ensuring that each component's outputs feed into downstream stages as inputs, respecting dependency constraints.

Advanced workflow composition embraces these capabilities:

- **Dynamic branching and conditional execution:** Pipelines can adapt execution paths based on parameter values or conditional criteria, such as early stopping upon performance thresholds.

- **Parallelism and concurrency:** Independent components or parameterized trials can be executed simultaneously to accelerate processing.

- **Subpipeline abstraction:** Complex workflows are decomposed into nested subpipelines, each composed of smaller modules, enhancing readability and maintainability.

- **Integration with orchestration platforms:** Workflow definition languages (e.g., Apache Airflow, Kubeflow Pipelines) enable automated scheduling, monitoring, and resource management.

For example, consider an image classification training pipeline where data augmentation, feature extraction, model training, and evaluation are modular stages. By parameterizing data augmentation intensity and model architectures, the pipeline can automatically execute a grid of experiments, each as a branch in the workflow DAG. This facilitates scalable experimentation while maintaining a unified pipeline definition.

Combining Parameterization and Modularity for Experiment Management

The interplay of parameterization and modularity yields pipelines that are not only reusable but also enable rich experiment management. Parameters govern behavior at the component level, enabling experimentation on hyperparameters or algorithm choices, while modularity ensures these components can be orchestrated seamlessly without code duplication.

Often, parameter configurations are stored externally in structured formats (e.g., YAML, JSON) or managed through experiment tracking systems. This separation enables versioning of parameters alongside model artifacts, creating a lineage trail critical for compliance and reproducibility.

```
def train_model(features, labels, learning_rate=0.01, epochs=10):
    model = initialize_model()
    optimizer = Optimizer(lr=learning_rate)
    for epoch in range(epochs):
        predictions = model(features)
        loss = compute_loss(predictions, labels)
        optimizer.step(loss)
    return model
```

Here, the function `train_model` abstracts training logic, exposing hyperparameters `learning_rate` and `epochs`. It can be invoked from different workflow scenarios with varying arguments without changing implementation, blending modularity and parameterization intrinsically.

Scaling Through Parameter-Driven Automation

Parameter-driven pipelines facilitate large-scale experimentation by automating configuration space exploration. Tools can instantiate multiple pipeline runs by enumerating parameter combinations or sampling parameter distributions, enabling hyperparameter optimization or ablation studies to be conducted systematically.

Such approaches reduce manual intervention and human error. Parallelism achieved through modular independent components further accelerates this process. The combination also supports continuous integration and deployment (CI/CD) workflows where model retraining is triggered automatically on new data or code changes, propagating parameterized adjustments consistently.

Summary of Best Practices

- Identify and externalize all variable elements in pipeline stages as explicit parameters.

- Design pipeline components with well-defined, minimal interfaces that articulate inputs, outputs, and configurable options.

- Construct DAGs that capture dependencies and support dynamic control flow for adaptive execution.

- Employ abstractions such as subpipelines or reusable modules to promote clarity and reduce redundancy.

- Leverage orchestration and experiment tracking frameworks that support parameter sweeps and automated reproducibility.

By mastering parameterization, modularity, and workflow composition, ML practitioners unlock advanced capabilities that translate into pipelines that are flexible, transparent, scalable, and robust, ultimately accelerating innovation and deployment in practical machine learning systems.

3.5. Custom Plugins and Execution Backends

Extending MLflow Projects through custom plugins and execution backends is instrumental in adapting the platform to novel computational environments and specialized workflows beyond native support. MLflow's modular architecture facilitates this extensibility, enabling users to integrate bespoke compute platforms, orchestrators, or resource managers while preserving the core capabilities of reproducible experimentation and model lifecycle management.

At the core of any extension is the `MLflow Projects` abstraction, which defines how projects are packaged, parameterized, and executed. Execution backends act as pluggable drivers translating these instructions into concrete tasks on infrastructure such as local machines, Kubernetes clusters, cloud platforms, or proprietary resource schedulers. The design pattern for custom backends centers on subclassing `mlflow.projects.ExecutionEnvironment` or closely related base classes, implementing the essential lifecycle interfaces for job submission, monitoring, and artifact handling.

Plugin Architecture and Discovery

A custom backend must conform to MLflow's plugin discovery model, which leverages Python entry points specified in `setup.py` or `pyproject.toml`. Registering an entry point under the `mlflow.projects.env` namespace enables MLflow's CLI and API to instantiate the backend dynamically when specified in the `mlflow run` command via the `--backend` flag. A typical entry point declaration resembles:

```
entry_points={
    'mlflow.projects.env': [
        'my_custom_backend = my_custom_module:MyCustomBackend',
    ],
},
```

When MLflow runs a project with `--backend my_custom_backend`, it imports `MyCustomBackend` and uses its interfaces to initiate execution. This mechanism unobtrusively integrates new compute environments without modifying core MLflow source code.

Key Interface Methods

Custom backends must implement foundational methods to manage the execution lifecycle:

- `run(...)`: Orchestrates the project execution including environment setup, parameter injection, and command invocation.

- `wait()`: Blocks until the project run completes on the remote or local execution environment.

- `cancel()`: Attempts to terminate the running job.

- `get_run_status()`: Returns the current execution state (e.g., RUNNING, FAILED, FINISHED).

- `get_run_uri()`: Provides the location where artifacts and logs can be accessed post-execution.

The `run()` method is typically the most complex, managing environment-specific authentication, resource allocation, container orchestration, and asynchronous job submission semantics compatible with the target infrastructure.

Handling Artifact and Log Access

Seamless integration requires the backend to expose artifact storage and logging consistently with MLflow's paradigm. For cloud or distributed compute environments, this often entails syncing artifacts back to an accessible remote store such as S3, Azure Blob Storage, or a shared filesystem. Custom backends should implement data transfer best practices and incremental syncing to minimize latency and bandwidth consumption.

Logging integration must ensure that stdout and stderr streams, as well as job meta-information like exit codes and error traces, are captured and retrievable via MLflow UI or API. Depending on capabilities, this may involve streaming logs through APIs or aggregating logs in centralized logging services.

Design Considerations for Robustness and Extensibility

Well-designed backends encapsulate environment-specific details cleanly, exposing consistent APIs and maintaining fault tolerance. Some recommended design tips include:

- **Idempotent and deterministic execution:** Ensure repeated invocations with the same parameters produce consistent results or cleanly handle partial failures or retries.

- **Asynchronous and event-driven patterns:** Support non-blocking job submission and efficient polling or callback-based status updates to scale with large workloads.

- **Credential and secrets management:** Abstract sensitive information handling through secure vaults or environment isolation, enabling seamless authentication.

- **Extensive logging and error propagation:** Surface meaningful diagnostics both locally and remotely to aid debugging and automated monitoring.

- **Parameter validation and sanitization:** Validate passed parameters early to prevent costly job failures due to invalid runtime inputs.

Moreover, backends should interoperate transparently with MLflow's existing artifact, metrics, and model logging APIs, facilitating end-to-end reproducibility and traceability.

Example: Kubernetes Execution Backend

A prominent example of a custom backend is one supporting Kubernetes clusters. The backend leverages Python Kubernetes client libraries to dynamically create and manage Pod specifications that mount source code, define runtime containers, and propagate project parameters as environment variables or command-line arguments. Asynchronous job submission via Kubernetes API enables non-blocking operation; periodic pod state polling informs status transitions. Logs are streamed from pod logs or aggregated using cluster logging stacks (e.g., Fluentd, Elasticsearch). Upon job completion, artifacts synced from persistent volumes or object storage buckets registered as volumes complete the integration.

```
class KubernetesBackend(ExecutionEnvironment):
    def run(self, uri, parameters, experiment_id, ...):
```

```
        pod_spec = self._create_pod_spec(uri, parameters)
        self.pod = self.k8s_client.create_namespaced_pod(pod_spec
   )
        return self

   def wait(self):
        while True:
            pod_status = self.k8s_client.
   read_namespaced_pod_status(self.pod.metadata.name)
            if pod_status.phase in ["Succeeded", "Failed"]:
                break
            time.sleep(self.poll_interval)

   def get_run_status(self):
        pod_status = self.k8s_client.read_namespaced_pod_status(
   self.pod.metadata.name)
        return pod_status.phase.upper()
```

While this snippet highlights core structure, real deployments incorporate additional logic for RBAC permissions, resource quotas, context propagation, and artifact synchronization.

Testing and Validation Strategies

Thorough testing is crucial to guarantee reliability across diverse deployment scenarios. Unit tests should mock external APIs and confirm that state transitions and error handling are correct. Integration tests involve deploying on test clusters or staging environments mirroring production configurations. Continuous integration pipelines automating these validations accelerate development and maintain quality.

Community and Contribution Practices

As MLflow evolves, contributing custom backends back to the community fosters broader compatibility and accelerates feature parity across compute environments. Following MLflow's coding guidelines, documenting all interfaces, and providing examples enhances maintainability and usability. Registering plugins with publicly accessible packages streamlines adoption.

Custom plugins and execution backends significantly expand MLflow Projects' applicability, enabling tailored compute integrations without sacrificing reproducibility or usability. By adhering to interface contracts, incorporating robust design patterns, and embracing modular architecture, developers can embed MLflow seamlessly into heterogeneous and complex machine learning infrastructure ecosystems.

3.6. Testing and Reproducibility in Production

Ensuring correctness and reproducibility at production scale is a foundational requirement for reliable systems in advanced technology environments. It demands a cohesive strategy that integrates comprehensive test coverage, automation pipelines, and real-world validation to guarantee that computational results remain consistent and auditable under evolving conditions.

At the core of reproducibility is deterministic execution-every production run must produce the same results given the same inputs, environment, and configuration. Achieving this necessitates meticulous versioning of source code, dependencies, data, and runtime parameters. Containerization and infrastructure-as-code practices enable consistent environments, minimizing discrepancies caused by underlying system changes. Immutable artifact generation, combined with cryptographic hashing, facilitates verification that inputs and outputs have not been altered inadvertently or maliciously.

Automated testing is the first line of defense in preventing regressions and verifying correctness. Unit tests isolate individual components to validate logic and interface contracts. Integration tests assure that combined modules interact correctly, reflecting the reality of complex production pipelines. End-to-end tests simulate entire workflows, offering assurance that the system's outputs meet functional expectations. In large-scale systems, test suites must be designed for parallel execution to maintain rapid feedback cycles.

Continuous integration (CI) systems orchestrate these tests automatically. Upon any code commit or configuration change, CI pipelines execute defined test sets, analyze results, and report deviations. Modern CI tools support artifact archival, environment provisioning, and can trigger downstream processes conditioned on test success. This automation reduces human error and shortens the cycle between development and reliable deployment.

Real-world edge cases often expose latent issues that synthetic tests can overlook. Incorporating production-like datasets, including corner cases derived from historical logs or stress scenarios, into test inputs improves robustness. Techniques such as fuzz testing introduce randomized perturbations that simulate unpredictable conditions or malformed inputs. These strategies highlight fault modes that might degrade system performance or correctness subtly.

To ensure faithful re-execution of production runs, comprehensive provenance capture must accompany each run. This involves recording metadata such as environment configuration, software versions, input data hashes, parameter settings, and execution traces. Provenance information must be stored securely and indexed for efficient retrieval and traceability over time. Queryable audit trails enable retrospective analysis, facilitating debugging, compliance verification, and replication of results months or years later.

In complex distributed systems, nondeterminism may arise due to concurrency, network variability, or hardware heterogeneity. Mitigation techniques include deterministic scheduling, controlled random seeds, and locking mechanisms to guarantee repeatable outcomes. When absolute determinism is unattainable, a well-defined tolerance threshold for variability should be established and tested rigorously.

Periodic regression testing in production environments is critical, especially when incremental updates or infrastructure changes are frequent. Canary releases and blue-green deployments can limit exposure by directing a subset of traffic to new versions and comparing outputs against stable baselines. Anomalies detected during these trials prompt rollback or targeted investigation before full rollout.

The following example illustrates an automated testing pipeline configuration using a continuous integration script with coverage for unit, integration, and fuzz tests:

```
#!/bin/bash
set -e

echo "Setting up environment..."
docker build -t myapp:test .

echo "Running unit tests..."
docker run --rm myapp:test ./run_unit_tests.sh

echo "Running integration tests..."
docker run --rm myapp:test ./run_integration_tests.sh

echo "Running fuzz tests on critical modules..."
docker run --rm myapp:test ./run_fuzz_tests.sh --iterations=10000

echo "Archiving test results and environment metadata..."
tar czf artifacts.tar.gz tests/results/ env_metadata.json

echo "Uploading artifacts to storage..."
aws s3 cp artifacts.tar.gz s3://my-ci-artifacts/$(date +%Y%m%d-%H
    %M%S)/

echo "Tests completed successfully."
```

The artifact archival includes environment metadata, such as container hashes, library versions, and configuration files, which are essential to reproduce the run at any subsequent time. This metadata can be generated during the build phase via commands like:

```
#!/bin/bash
echo "Capturing environment metadata..."
echo "Commit hash: $(git rev-parse HEAD)" > env_metadata.json
echo "Docker image digest: $(docker images --digests myapp:test)"
    >> env_metadata.json
echo "Installed packages:" >> env_metadata.json
```

```
dpkg -l >> env_metadata.json
```

The integration of comprehensive automated testing, continuous integration, and provenance capture supports a feedback mechanism that prevents regression ground-downs and enables continuous delivery with confidence. Additionally, carefully curated real-world edge scenario testing addresses the inevitable complexity and unpredictability inherent in production systems.

Beyond software, data inputs must also be subject to validation pipelines. Data drift detection, schema validation, and anomaly detection algorithms ensure that inputs remain within expected bounds and format. Such validation prevents silent degradation of results due to corrupted or shifted data landscapes.

Finally, auditing reproducibility necessitates retention policies that strike a balance between storage costs and long-term accessibility. Archiving raw inputs, logs, execution environments, and output artifacts in cold storage, potentially with cryptographic timestamping, ensures tamper-evident traceability. Enterprise solutions may combine metadata registries, immutable ledger technologies, and formal verification tools to satisfy stringent regulatory or compliance regimes.

Altogether, these strategies build a resilient ecosystem in which production runs are reproducible, auditable, and correct. They enable organizations to identify, isolate, and resolve faults rapidly, improve system trustworthiness, and maintain operational excellence in a continuous evolution landscape.

Chapter 4

Model Packaging, Validation, and Deployment

Step beyond experimentation and bring your models to life—safely, scalably, and reproducibly. This chapter unravels how MLflow makes model packaging seamless, ensures validation and compliance, and unlocks powerful deployment workflows across diverse targets, including clouds, clusters, and edge devices. Discover how to avoid deployment pitfalls, automate model delivery, and operationalize machine learning with confidence.

4.1. MLflow Model Flavors and pyfunc Interface

MLflow's design philosophy centers on simplifying and standardizing the management of machine learning models across myriad frameworks and deployment environments. Central to this approach is the concept of *model flavors*, which abstract the peculiarities of different machine learning libraries and provide a uniform interface for model serialization, deployment, and inference. This abstraction is complemented by the `pyfunc` interface, a universal Python-based wrapper that allows custom models to coexist seamlessly within the MLflow ecosystem.

MLflow's support for multiple model flavors enables users to log and serve models built with diverse machine learning frameworks, including but not limited to Scikit-learn, TensorFlow, and PyTorch. Each flavor encapsulates the model artifacts in a format native to its originating framework while adhering to MLflow's standardized directory structure and metadata specification.

Scikit-learn Flavor The Scikit-learn flavor serializes models using Python's `pickle` mechanism, preserving the entire pipeline object graph encapsulated by Scikit-learn's `Pipeline` and estimator classes. Specifically, MLflow stores a serialized file (generally `model.pkl`) that can be loaded directly with Scikit-learn's `joblib` or `pickle` utilities. Logging a Scikit-learn model with MLflow automatically records all metadata, including model parameters, signatures, and environment dependencies, facilitating precise reproducibility. During deployment, MLflow's Scikit-learn flavor ensures that the serving container has access to the exact Python environment used for training, thereby minimizing runtime discrepancies.

TensorFlow Flavor TensorFlow models, often exported as `SavedModel` bundles, are supported natively by MLflow. When logging TensorFlow models, MLflow archives the entire computational graph, including variables, meta-information, and signature definitions, consistent with TensorFlow's standard model artifact structure. Importantly, MLflow captures the serving signatures, which delineate the model's input and output tensors, thereby enabling robust validation and schema enforcement during deployment. By leveraging TensorFlow's serving standards within its flavor, MLflow guarantees compatibility with TensorFlow Serving and other deployment platforms consuming SavedModel artifacts.

PyTorch Flavor The PyTorch flavor in MLflow supports both scripted and traced models, leveraging TorchScript for model serialization. Models logged with this flavor are saved using torch.jit.save, producing a self-contained artifact that encodes the entire model topology along with its parameters. This approach preserves the dynamic computational graph characteristics unique to PyTorch, while making the models portable and framework-agnostic at runtime. Furthermore, MLflow manages dependency versions and environment specifications, ensuring that the PyTorch runtime during deployment mirrors the training context.

While framework-specific flavors optimize for native model storage and serving, the pyfunc interface acts as a lingua franca for model integration in MLflow's ecosystem. The pyfunc flavor defines a standard Python function interface that all models must implement for inference compatibility. This design introduces a critical abstraction: regardless of the underlying framework, a model adhering to pyfunc can be loaded and served consistently by MLflow.

The core requirement for a pyfunc model is the implementation of a predict method accepting a pandas.DataFrame as input and producing either a pandas.DataFrame or a numpy.ndarray as output. This uniform signature level-sets model invocation semantics, simplifying integration with downstream applications and validation pipelines.

Creating Custom pyfunc Wrappers To integrate models from unsupported or proprietary frameworks, or to customize pre- and post-processing logic, MLflow users can extend the pyfunc.PythonModel base class. This requires implementing the predict method encapsulating inference behavior. The wrapper class handles inputs and outputs in the standardized format, while internally managing framework-specific model calls.

```
import mlflow.pyfunc
import pandas as pd

class CustomModelWrapper(mlflow.pyfunc.PythonModel):
    def load_context(self, context):
        import some_framework
        self.model = some_framework.load_model(context.artifacts
    ["model_path"])

    def predict(self, context, model_input: pd.DataFrame) -> pd.
    DataFrame:
        preds = self.model.predict(model_input.values)
        return pd.DataFrame(preds, columns=["predictions"])
```

Users then package the wrapper along with required artifacts and environment specifications using MLflow's logging APIs, which preserve portability and reproducibility.

The synergy between built-in flavors and the `pyfunc` interface constitutes a powerful mechanism for model interoperability. By exporting models in native artifacts alongside their `pyfunc` representation, MLflow allows different flavors to be abstracted under a consistent runtime interface. This enables, for example, a TensorFlow model to be consumed by a generic Python-based inference service without requiring specialized TensorFlow code, as the `pyfunc` layer standardizes input/output handling.

From a testing perspective, the `pyfunc` abstraction streamlines unit and integration tests by enabling evaluation scripts to interact with any MLflow-logged model through a uniform method. This eliminates the need for framework-specific test harnesses and reduces code complexity. Validation pipelines can automatically verify conformance to input schema, output format, and model accuracy irrespective of the underlying model flavor.

Moreover, MLflow's abstraction minimizes the need for users to deeply understand the idiosyncrasies of each machine learning framework when deploying or serving models. It also facilitates

84

seamless transitions between experiment tracking, model registry, and deployment stages, unifying the MLOps process.

Flavor	Serialization Format	Primary Use Case
Scikit-learn	Pickled Pipeline/Estimator	Classical ML pipelines, low-latency serving
TensorFlow	TensorFlow SavedModel	Deep learning with flexible serving signatures
PyTorch	TorchScript (.pt files)	Dynamic graph models, custom architectures
pyfunc	Python wrapper with standardized predict	Framework-agnostic inference, custom models

The design of MLflow's model flavors and the pyfunc interface exemplifies a balanced approach that embraces framework-specific strengths while enforcing a consistent API contract. This enables practitioners to leverage the best capabilities of each framework, integrated smoothly into enterprise-grade machine learning workflows.

4.2. Artifact Management and Serialization

The effective management and serialization of machine learning artifacts are critical for ensuring reproducibility, scalability, and maintainability of model deployment workflows. Artifacts encompass everything from trained models and preprocessing pipelines to configuration files and data transformation scripts, all of which constitute the inference assets necessary for consistent and reliable model operation. This section provides an in-depth examination of techniques and best practices to structure, manage, serialize, and version these components across heterogeneous storage backends.

Artifact Cataloging and Typing

Central to artifact management is an organized catalog system that classifies and indexes artifacts according to their role in the model lifecycle. Key artifact types typically include:

- **Model binaries and checkpoints:** Serialized weights

and architectures necessary for inference and retraining.

- **Data preprocessing artifacts:** Feature encoders, normalizers, and transformers.

- **Configuration:** Hyperparameters, environment specifications, and runtime options.

- **Metadata:** Provenance, training metrics, and lineage information.

- **Auxiliary code:** Custom layers or utilities that complement the model.

A well-defined metadata schema describing each artifact's type, creation timestamp, version identifiers, and dependencies facilitates automation in artifact discovery, retrieval, and validation. This schema serves as the backbone of both local and distributed artifact stores, enabling traceability and impact analysis over the models and their components.

Serialization Techniques

Serialization transforms in-memory objects-including trained models, parameters, and pre/post-processing modules-into byte streams suitable for persistent storage or transmission. The choice of serialization format hinges on factors such as supported data structures, cross-platform compatibility, ease of inspection, and storage efficiency. Prominent serialization formats in machine learning pipelines include:

- **Protocol Buffers and FlatBuffers:** Schema-based, highly efficient serialization optimized for speed and compactness, suitable for low-latency environments.

- **ONNX (Open Neural Network Exchange):** An open format capturing both model topology and weights, enabling cross-framework interoperability.

86

- **Pickle (Python-specific):** Flexible and easy for experiments, but carries security risks and limited portability.

- **HDF5 and TensorFlow SavedModel:** Hierarchical formats capable of encapsulating weights, metadata, and graph information for complex artifacts.

Serialization is often complemented by compression (for example, using gzip or LZ4) to reduce storage footprint, particularly when managing large ensembles or multiple versions.

Dependency Management

Model artifacts rarely function in isolation. Reproducibility depends on capturing precise versions of libraries, framework runtimes, and hardware configurations used during training and inference. Strategies for encapsulating dependencies include:

- **Environment specification files:** Declarative formats such as `requirements.txt`, `environment.yml` or Dockerfiles declaring explicit package versions.

- **Containerization:** Docker or similar images bundle code, dependencies, and runtime environments, ensuring fidelity across deployment targets.

- **Virtual environments and snapshots:** Tools like Conda or virtualenv lock Python package versions and can be serialized and shared alongside the model artifact.

Effective pipelines embed environment hashes or manifests within artifact metadata to enable downstream verification.

Versioning Strategies

Robust versioning uniquely identifies every artifact instance and tracks changes systematically. Common approaches include:

- **Semantic versioning:** Using `MAJOR.MINOR.PATCH` schemes to communicate compatibility guarantees.

- **Content-addressable storage (CAS):** Indexing artifacts by cryptographic hash values computed over their content, yielding immutable, collision-resistant identifiers.

- **Git-based versioning:** Leveraging Git repositories for source code, configuration and small models enables diffing, branching, and history tracking.

- **Artifact registries and model hubs:** Platforms such as MLflow Model Registry, TensorBoard HParams or Hugging Face Model Hub provide built-in support for artifact versioning, lifecycle states and lineage visualization.

Integration between version control systems and artifact stores enables CI/CD pipelines to automate testing, promotion and rollback of model artifacts.

Diverse Artifact Stores

Storage solutions must accommodate diverse access patterns and scalability requirements:

- **Object storage systems:** Amazon S3, Google Cloud Storage and Azure Blob Storage offer durable, scalable blob storage with lifecycle policies and event triggers.

- **Network and distributed file systems:** NFS, Ceph or HDFS provide shared-access, POSIX-compliant interfaces suitable for large-scale training environments.

- **Database-backed stores:** Key-value stores (for example, Redis or DynamoDB) or specialized artifact repositories (for example, JFrog Artifactory) add metadata indexing and fine-grained access control.

- **On-premises vaults:** Enterprise solutions often adopt hybrid approaches incorporating compliance and encryption standards.

Combining these with caching layers or content delivery networks optimizes model loading performance during inference. Effective integration ensures fault tolerance, atomic updates and audit trails.

End-to-End Artifact Workflow

A canonical artifact management workflow integrates serialization, dependency capture, versioning and storage as follows:

1. Serialize the model and associated artifacts using a standardized format (for example, ONNX or SavedModel).

2. Generate detailed metadata capturing artifact type, origin, environment hashes and dependency manifests.

3. Compute content hashes to enforce immutability and enable CAS indexing.

4. Store artifacts in a chosen artifact store with appropriate access controls and retention policies.

5. Register artifact versions in a model registry system, linking versions to training runs and evaluation metrics.

6. Trigger promotions of artifact versions through development, staging and production stages.

7. Monitor artifact lineage and dependency integrity to detect incompatibilities or drift.

This pipeline ensures artifacts remain consistent and traceable from development through deployment, mitigating pitfalls such as environment mismatch, silent drift or undocumented changes.

Challenges and Best Practices

Artifact management faces several challenges inherent to the complexity and dynamism of machine learning ecosystems:

- **Heterogeneity:** Supporting multiple frameworks, serialization formats and runtime environments requires extensible and modular artifact schemas.

- **Granularity tradeoffs:** Balancing artifact granularity (monolithic models versus modular components) impacts transfer and storage overheads.

- **Security and compliance:** Artifacts may contain sensitive data or intellectual property, necessitating encryption, access controls and audit mechanisms.

- **Scalability:** Large-scale model provenance demands high-throughput indexing, replication and disaster recovery strategies.

Adopting standardized artifact schemas, leveraging containerization and employing model registries with built-in version control are foundational steps toward addressing these complexities. Embedding artifact management into CI/CD pipelines and governance workflows accelerates adoption and operational maturity. The integration of disciplined artifact serialization, comprehensive dependency encapsulation, robust versioning and reliable storage constitutes the core of scalable, reproducible and maintainable model lifecycle management, enabling organizations to build auditable machine learning production systems that withstand evolving data and environments.

4.3. Model Validation and Testing

Effective model validation and testing are indispensable pillars in the machine learning lifecycle, ensuring that models perform reliably and safely once deployed. This section explicates the crucial steps and methodologies required to validate models rigorously before deployment, focusing on signature enforcement, input/output schema management, performance testing, regression checks, and the integration of quality gates into deployment pipelines.

Signature Enforcement

A model signature defines the explicit contract for a model's inputs and outputs, specifying data types, shapes, and semantics. Enforcing model signature validation constitutes the first line of defense against incompatible or malformed data during production inference. The signature encapsulates necessary metadata such as feature names, expected data types (e.g., integers, floats, categorical), tensor dimensions, and permissible value ranges.

Strong signature enforcement guarantees that any input deviating from the defined contract triggers a validation failure, preventing erroneous or corrupt data from polluting both inference outcomes and downstream systems. Validation frameworks or serving platforms typically employ automated checks validating input shapes against expected dimensions and data types prior to request forwarding. Similarly, outputs are validated to conform to defined ranges or enumerations, enabling early detection of anomalies such as model degradation or logic faults.

Input/Output Schema Management

Managing robust schemas for both inputs and outputs is essential to maintain data integrity and facilitate versioning control. Schema management encompasses the formal specification, storage, and evolution of data definitions. An extensible schema framework accommodates iterative feature enhancements, new output metrics, or format adjustments without disrupting services.

Tools supporting schema evolution allow compatibility checks that alert developers when changes introduce backward incompatibility, such as removing or renaming input features. This foresight is paramount in collaborative environments or continuous integration scenarios to avoid silent failures after deployment. Moreover, schemas enable automatic generation of validation tests and provide documentation artifacts for data engineers and consumers.

Typically, schemas are expressed in languages such as JSON Schema, Apache Avro, or Protocol Buffers, which facilitate machine-readable specification and integration with validation libraries. Embedding schema validation inside model serving infrastructure reinforces the safeguard that each inference call adheres to expected semantics.

Performance Testing

Performance testing evaluates the model's operational characteristics and predictive quality under expected and edge-case conditions. This testing goes beyond standard training-validation accuracy metrics to incorporate latency profiling, throughput measurements, and resource utilization on deployment hardware.

Rigorous performance benchmarking includes stress tests by simulating high-concurrency inference requests, along with input distributions that mimic real-world variations and anomalies. These tests help confirm that the model meets application-specific service-level objectives (SLOs) such as maximum latency, minimal memory footprint, and consistent throughput.

Additionally, performance testing comprises detailed predictive quality analysis using holdout datasets that represent production data. Metrics such as precision, recall, F1-score, area under the ROC curve, mean squared error, or custom business KPIs are systematically calculated and compared against baseline thresholds. These metrics must be contextualized relative to the data distribution, class balance, and potential bias to ensure fairness and optimal generalization.

Regression Checks

Regression testing is fundamental to detect unwanted degradation or behavioral changes in the model's predictions following updates, retraining, or feature engineering modifications. This process involves re-evaluation of the new model against a comprehensive suite of regression test cases designed to monitor stability and correctness.

Automated regression tests leverage carefully curated datasets that emphasize critical edge cases, rare event scenarios, and business-sensitive segments. The model's predictions on these datasets are compared with those from the prior production model. Any statistically significant deviations or drops in key metrics must trigger alerts and block deployment until resolved.

Regression checks can also include statistical distribution comparisons-often referred to as data drift or concept drift detection-to identify shifts in data patterns that might impair predictive validity. Sophisticated regression pipelines integrate threshold-based anomaly detection algorithms to quantify and interpret deviations.

Embedding Quality Gates in Deployment Pipelines

Integrating quality gates into continuous integration and continuous deployment (CI/CD) pipelines encapsulates best practices to enforce model robustness before release. Quality gates serve as automated checkpoints that assess model artifacts against predefined validation criteria, typically including signature compliance, schema adherence, performance benchmarks, and regression test pass rates.

These gates may be implemented as scripted validation jobs or orchestrated with workflow tools, ensuring that models failing any validation step are automatically rejected from further deployment stages. Logging and reporting mechanisms document validation outcomes, facilitating traceability and auditability.

Embedding quality gates early in the pipeline accelerates feedback loops for data scientists and engineers, promoting proactive remediation of issues. Moreover, it establishes reproducible and transparent deployment protocols that align with governance and regulatory requirements.

The collective application of signature enforcement, schema management, comprehensive performance testing, rigorous regression checks, and automated quality gates is imperative to deploy machine learning models with confidence. These practices minimize risks related to data inconsistencies, runtime failures, and performance erosion, thus enabling reliable, scalable, and maintainable model-driven systems.

4.4. Exporting, Importing, and Migrating MLflow Models

MLflow's architecture facilitates the seamless movement of machine learning models across diverse environments, ensuring consistent reproducibility, scalability, and traceability. Effective export, import, and migration strategies are central to enabling interoperability between local development environments, cloud infrastructures, and third-party platforms without loss of metadata or lineage.

MLflow models are encapsulated in a standardized directory structure consisting of the model's serialized artifacts, conda or pip environment specifications, and an `MLmodel` descriptor file. This structure provides a self-contained representation, allowing models to be reliably transported and deployed.

Model Export

Exporting a model involves packaging the MLflow model directory for transfer or archival. This is routinely achieved by saving the model with the `mlflow.pyfunc.save_model()` API or exporting an existing run's model artifact.

```
import mlflow.pyfunc

# Assuming a trained model and run context
model_path = "/tmp/mlflow_exported_model"
mlflow.pyfunc.save_model(path=model_path, python_model=model)
```

The saved directory contains:

- `MLmodel`: A YAML descriptor specifying flavors, signatures, and metadata.

- Model data files: Serialized model weights and supporting binaries.

- Environment files: `conda.yaml` or `requirements.txt`, capturing dependencies.

Archive this directory (e.g., tarball or zip) to facilitate transport to remote environments, or directly upload it to a cloud object store connected with MLflow's artifact repository.

Model Import

Importing a model requires retrieving the model artifacts and restoring the original environment and metadata. MLflow's `mlflow.pyfunc.load_model()` provides transparent access:

```
import mlflow.pyfunc

model_uri = "runs:/<run_id>/model"
loaded_model = mlflow.pyfunc.load_model(model_uri)
```

```
# The model_uri can also point to
# - local filesystem paths
# - cloud storage URIs (s3://, gs://, abfs://)
# - registered MLflow model versions (models:/<name>/<stage>)
```

MLflow automatically resolves and recreates the conda or pip environment specified, ensuring runtime consistency. To enable this, the target environment must have compatible Python versions and access to the dependency specification files, which MLflow uses to instantiate isolated environments.

Cross-Environment Model Migration

Migrating MLflow models between heterogeneous environments demands careful handling of artifact repositories, environment replication, and metadata preservation.

Metadata and Lineage Preservation MLflow's core strength lies in maintaining comprehensive metadata and lineage. Each model version is linked to training runs logged in the MLflow tracking server, which records parameters, metrics, tags, and source code references. When migrating a model, the following must be preserved to retain full traceability:

- `MLmodel` descriptor: Ensures flavor and signature consistency.

- Run metadata: Parameters and metrics logged with the model.

- Source code snapshot or Git commit hash.

- Artifact versions and dependencies.

Transferring the entire MLflow tracking server database and artifact repository is often necessary for complete traceability across environments.

Artifact Repository Synchronization Models frequently depend on artifacts stored in locations such as S3 buckets, Azure Blob Storage, or Google Cloud Storage. When migrating models, it is crucial to synchronize artifact repositories between the source and target environments:

- Replicate object store contents using cloud-native CLI tools (`aws s3 sync`, `azcopy`, `gsutil`).

- Update MLflow tracking server artifact root URIs accordingly.

- Maintain consistent folder structures and access policies.

Environment Reproduction Ensuring reproducible environments requires transferring environment specifications and recreating isolated environments on the destination system. MLflow's environment files enable this:

- Use `conda.yaml` for conda environments: execute `conda env create -f conda.yaml`.

- Use `requirements.txt` for pip environments: execute `pip install -r requirements.txt`.

In containerized deployments, the model folder and `MLmodel` metadata can be embedded within Docker images, facilitating immutable migration.

Migration to and from Cloud Environments

Modern workflows increasingly leverage cloud-managed MLflow services or cloud-native artifact stores. Migrating models between on-premises setups and cloud environments involves these considerations:

- **Authentication and Access Control**: Ensure that the MLflow tracking servers and artifact repositories have compatible authentication mechanisms. Configure appropriate role-based access controls for secure artifact and metadata transfer.

- **Model Registry Synchronization**: Cloud MLflow Model Registry implementations support version tracking and stage transitions. When migrating, export registered models using the MLflow CLI or REST API, and import them to target registries, preserving version and stage annotations.

- **URI Translation**: Artifact URIs may need rewriting to reflect different storage paths (e.g., changing s3:// to file:// or vice versa).

Interoperability with Third-Party Platforms

MLflow's model format supports standardized flavors such as PyFunc, TensorFlow SavedModel, ONNX, and H2O. This standardization enables integration and migration across frameworks and platforms:

- Export models in a flavor native to the target platform, e.g., mlflow.tensorflow.save_model() for TensorFlow Serving.

- When importing from external systems, convert or wrap models to conform to MLflow's MLmodel format using custom pyfunc wrappers.

- Retain serialized signatures and input/output schema in the metadata for accurate API serving and validation across systems.

Example: Model Migration Workflow

Assume migrating a model from a local development machine to a cloud MLflow tracking server with an S3 artifact store.

1. Export the model locally:

```
mlflow models export --run-id <run_id> --output /tmp/
exported_model
```

2. Upload exported artifacts to S3:

```
aws s3 cp /tmp/exported_model s3://my-mlflow-artifacts/
path --recursive
```

3. Register the model in the cloud MLflow model registry:

```
mlflow models register -m s3://my-mlflow-artifacts/path
/MLmodel -n MyModel
```

4. On the cloud environment, load the model preserving environment:

```
model = mlflow.pyfunc.load_model("models:/MyModel/
Production")
```

This workflow ensures full reproducibility, traceability, and smooth operational integration.

The crux of successful export, import, and migration in MLflow rests on preserving the fidelity of model artifacts, environment specifications, and the rich metadata framework. Combining MLflow's intrinsic capabilities with best practices concerning artifact and environment synchronization yields robust, reproducible cross-environment workflows vital for enterprise-scale ML operations.

4.5. Model Serving with MLflow

MLflow provides a comprehensive framework to serve machine learning models in diverse production environments. It supports multiple serving modalities including REST APIs for low-latency online inference, batch endpoints for processing large datasets asynchronously, and real-time interfaces for high-throughput streaming applications. Understanding these options and their deployment implications is essential for building robust, scalable, and maintainable model serving architectures.

Serving via MLflow REST API

MLflow's REST API enables immediate deployment of models as HTTP endpoints, allowing external clients to request predictions with minimal overhead. Once a model is logged and registered within MLflow's Model Registry, serving can be initiated using the built-in MLflow Models serving server:

```
mlflow models serve -m models:/<model_name>/<stage> -p 5000 --no-
    conda
```

This command starts a REST API server on port 5000 for the specified registered model stage (e.g., "Production"). The server exposes a /invocations endpoint accepting JSON payloads with input features, returning inference results in JSON format. This setup is ideal for development, experimentation, or latency-sensitive applications where immediate responses (on the order of milliseconds to a few seconds) are critical.

For production, it is common to front the MLflow serving API with a reverse proxy or API gateway that manages request routing, authentication, and throttling. Commonly, Kubernetes ingress controllers or cloud-native load balancers integrate with MLflow serving replicas to enable horizontal scaling. The REST API interface's simplicity allows easy integration with existing HTTP-based workflows, simplifying DevOps and application deployment.

Batch Endpoints for Asynchronous Inference

Many real-world use cases necessitate bulk scoring of large datasets where real-time response is not paramount. MLflow supports batch model inference either through orchestrated jobs that query the model artifact and apply inference over datasets or through prebuilt connectors in MLflow Projects combined with cloud batch processing services.

A typical batch serving pattern involves:

- Extracting feature data in bulk from data lakes or warehouses.

- Loading the MLflow model artifact as a local Python object.

- Applying model transformations and outputting scored results.

- Writing these results back to a persistent store for downstream analytics or reporting.

Batch workflows naturally decouple prediction latency from inference volume, enabling scalability to millions of records without impacting online system performance. They are best orchestrated via workflow management tools (e.g., Apache Airflow, Kubeflow Pipelines), which can invoke MLflow Projects or Python scripts incorporating MLflow's model loading APIs.

```
import mlflow.pyfunc
model = mlflow.pyfunc.load_model("models:/<model_name>/<stage>")
input_data = load_large_dataset()
predictions = model.predict(input_data)
save_predictions(predictions)
```

This approach offers flexibility and independence from serving infrastructure constraints but lacks immediate feedback, making it suitable for offline analytics or large-scale recommendation systems.

Real-Time Interfaces and Streaming Integration

For applications demanding continuous, high-throughput, and low-latency predictions (e.g., fraud detection, clickstream analysis), MLflow's serving can be embedded within streaming pipelines. Although MLflow does not natively provide streaming serving endpoints, model artifacts exported via MLflow can be deployed within streaming frameworks like Apache Flink, Kafka Streams, or custom microservices.

One effective pattern is to containerize the MLflow model within a microservice exposing a gRPC or RESTful API, integrated into a streaming architecture such as:

- Consuming streaming data from Kafka topics or other messaging systems.

- Performing real-time inference per message through the microservice.

- Emitting enriched results downstream for aggregation or alerting.

This model promotes low-latency inference with robust backpressure and fault tolerance governed by the streaming platform, while still leveraging MLflow's flexible model management.

Deployment Patterns: Latency, Scalability, and High Availability

Selecting an appropriate serving pattern depends on critical production requirements: inference latency tolerance, throughput scaling, and uptime guarantees. MLflow's serving architecture can be adapted into various deployment topologies:

- **Single-instance Serving:** A simple deployment involves running MLflow model serving on a single host. While straightforward, it represents a single point of failure and offers limited scalability, suitable only for low-demand or experimental use cases.

- **Load-balanced Multi-instance Serving:** To address scalability and availability, multiple MLflow serving instances can run behind a load balancer (e.g., Nginx, Envoy, or cloud provider load balancers). The load balancer distributes incoming inference requests evenly, enabling horizontal scaling and throughput improvements.

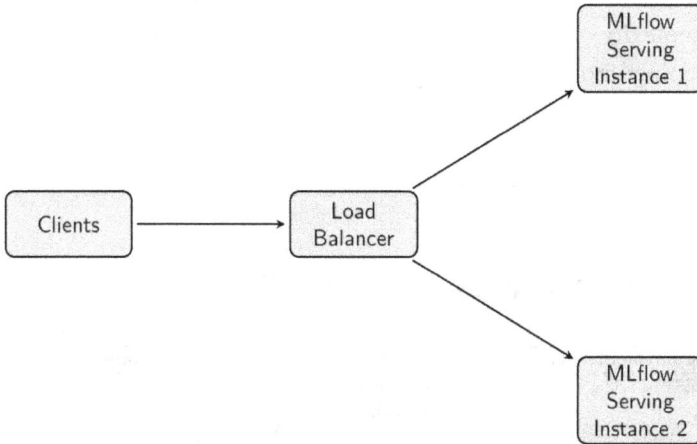

This pattern ensures that high incoming volumes do not overwhelm a single instance. Health checks and automatic instance replacement mechanisms provided by orchestration platforms (e.g., Kubernetes) improve resilience.

- **Failover and Redundancy:** High-availability setups require mechanisms to detect instance failures and reroute traffic. Load balancers configured with health probes can automatically exclude unhealthy instances. For mission-critical deployments, active-active cluster configurations combined with distributed storage of model artifacts ensure continuous availability.

- **Model Versioning and Canary Deployments:** MLflow's Model Registry facilitates smooth transitions between model versions by allowing staged rollouts. Canary deployments direct a fraction of traffic to new versions under monitoring, reducing risk. Load balancers or API gateways can route requests based on defined traffic splits.

Latency Considerations

Inference latency is influenced predominantly by model complexity, serving infrastructure, and network overhead. Keeping models lightweight, employing efficient serialization formats (e.g., ONNX), and enabling model warm starts reduce response times. Container orchestration systems can autoscale serving instances based on request metrics to maintain latency SLAs.

Summary of Deployment Trade-offs

Deployment Mode	Strengths	Limitations
REST API Single Instance	Simple, low setup overhead, minimal latency	No redundancy, limited scalability
Load-balanced REST API	Scalable, high availability	Requires orchestration, slightly higher latency
Batch Endpoints	Handles large volumes, cost-effective at scale	High latency, no real-time feedback
Streaming Integration	Real-time, scalable, fault-tolerant	Complex integration, higher operational overhead

MLflow's serving capabilities offer flexible options adaptable to the unique needs of applications ranging from experimental inference to enterprise-grade production deployments. Combining MLflow's registry, serving, and integration patterns with robust orchestration and load balancing enables production ML systems that fulfill stringent latency, scalability, and high-availability requirements.

4.6. Integration with Serving Infrastructures

Integration of MLflow models into large-scale serving infrastructures is a critical step toward operationalizing machine learning (ML) workflows in enterprise environments. Serving infrastructures such as Kubernetes, Amazon SageMaker, Microsoft Azure Machine Learning, and edge computing platforms each introduce unique considerations for deployment, monitoring, and lifecycle management. This section explores patterns and tactics to effectively leverage MLflow models within these environments, emphasizing production-grade reliability, scalability, and maintainability.

Deployment Patterns in Kubernetes

Kubernetes has become the de facto standard for orchestrating containerized applications in cloud-native environments. MLflow models, typically packaged as self-contained Docker images or served through MLflow's built-in serving capabilities, can be deployed as Kubernetes Pods within managed clusters. The recommended pattern employs Kubernetes Deployments combined with horizontal pod autoscalers (HPAs) to handle variable inference workloads.

A canonical workflow involves containerizing the MLflow model serving stack-potentially including custom pre- and post-processing logic-using a Dockerfile that installs the MLflow runtime, loads the model artifact, and exposes an HTTP API via MLflow's `mlflow models serve` interface or a customized FastAPI/Flask application. This container image is then deployed with a Kubernetes Deployment manifest specifying resource requests, limits, and environment variables for dynamic configuration.

To ensure production-grade scalability, an HPA monitors pod resource utilization (CPU, memory) or custom application metrics exposed via Prometheus. This setup enables automatic scaling: when inference request rates increase, new pods spin up, and when traffic diminishes, pods scale down to conserve resources. Networking configurations, including ingress controllers or service meshes like Istio, facilitate routing, authentication, and load balancing, contributing to secure and reliable serving endpoints.

```
apiVersion: apps/v1
kind: Deployment
metadata:
  name: mlflow-model
spec:
  replicas: 2
```

```
selector:
  matchLabels:
    app: mlflow-model
template:
  metadata:
    labels:
      app: mlflow-model
  spec:
    containers:
    - name: mlflow-server
      image: myregistry/mlflow-model:latest
      ports:
      - containerPort: 5000
      resources:
        requests:
          cpu: "500m"
          memory: "1Gi"
        limits:
          cpu: "1"
          memory: "2Gi"
      env:
      - name: MLFLOW_MODEL_URI
        value: "models:/MyModel/Production"
```

Deployment on Managed Cloud Platforms: SageMaker and AzureML

Managed ML serving platforms such as Amazon SageMaker and Microsoft AzureML provide end-to-end solutions for serving MLflow models, abstracting away much of infrastructure management while offering native integration with cloud storage, security, and monitoring services. MLflow's model format flexibility ensures smooth compatibility with these platforms.

In SageMaker, an MLflow model can be exported as a Docker-compatible model archive and deployed as a SageMaker endpoint with built-in autoscaling and A/B testing capabilities. This requires building a serving container that complies with SageMaker's inference specification, typically extending the MLflow PyFunc flavor or utilizing SageMaker's script mode for custom inference logic. SageMaker handles load balancing, canary deployments, rollback, and integrates with CloudWatch for real-time monitoring of inference latency, error rates, and throughput.

106

AzureML supports MLflow models through its model registry and deployment mechanisms, enabling direct deployment from MLflow model URIs into Azure Container Instances, Azure Kubernetes Service, or Azure Functions. AzureML pipelines facilitate lifecycle management with automated retraining, versioning, and monitoring via Application Insights, offering telemetry on health metrics and usage patterns. The platform supports secure key vault integration for managing secrets and tokens required during inference.

Edge Deployment Considerations

Edge serving presents additional constraints due to limited computational resources, intermittent connectivity, and latency sensitivity. Deploying MLflow models at the edge necessitates optimization of model size, efficient serialization formats such as ONNX or TensorRT, and lightweight serving frameworks.

One viable pattern involves exporting MLflow models to portable formats compatible with edge runtimes, such as TensorFlow Lite or ONNX Runtime, then wrapping inference logic in minimal containerized or standalone binaries. Devices can load models locally and expose inference endpoints through lightweight HTTP servers. Model updates employ over-the-air (OTA) mechanisms, leveraging edge orchestration frameworks to synchronize model versions securely and atomically.

Robust monitoring at the edge often combines local telemetry aggregation with periodic synchronization to centralized monitoring platforms to preserve bandwidth and ensure compliance with enterprise governance. Lifecycle management at the edge also incorporates fallback mechanisms and can leverage model quantization or pruning strategies to maintain performance within hardware constraints.

Production-Grade Monitoring and Lifecycle Management

Across all serving infrastructures, integrated model monitoring and lifecycle management are paramount. Effective monitoring involves continuous tracking of both system metrics (CPU, memory, network latency) and ML-specific metrics such as prediction distributions, input feature drift, output confidence scores, and error rates. MLflow Models can be instrumented to emit such telemetry by integrating hooks into the inference pipeline or leveraging middlewares that intercept request-response cycles.

Centralized monitoring platforms-including Prometheus, Grafana, AWS CloudWatch, or Azure Monitor-enable aggregation, alerting, and dashboarding of these metrics, supporting anomaly detection and triggering automated retraining workflows. Data drift detection and concept drift detection pipelines can be constructed using model explainability frameworks combined with production data.

Lifecycle management encompasses version control, staged rollouts, rollback capabilities, and automated retraining. MLflow's model registry supports versioning and stage transitions, promoting systematic promotion of models from staging to production. Blue-green deployment and canary testing patterns minimize downtime and reduce risk by directing subsets of traffic to new model versions while observing performance.

Automated retraining can be orchestrated through pipeline frameworks that trigger model retraining based on monitoring signals or predefined schedules, followed by validation and redeployment. Integration with CI/CD systems ensures rigorous testing before production release, while infrastructure-as-code tools codify deployment artifacts for reproducibility.

Security and Compliance Considerations

Serving MLflow models in enterprise environments demands attention to security and compliance. Serving endpoints should enforce authentication and authorization policies, often implemented via API gateways or identity-aware proxies. Sensitive data handling requires encryption in transit and at rest, secure secret management, and audit logging.

Kubernetes namespaces or cloud service roles segregate access between environments, and model artifacts must be scanned for vulnerabilities or embedded artifacts. Compliance with standards such as GDPR or HIPAA may influence deployment architectures-for example, enforcing data locality on edge devices or cloud regions.

Integrating MLflow models into diverse serving infrastructures is a multifaceted endeavor requiring alignment of containerization, orchestration, monitoring, scaling, security, and lifecycle automation. By adopting established patterns tailored to each infrastructure's unique capabilities and constraints, enterprises can achieve resilient and scalable ML services capable of supporting mission-critical applications at scale.

Chapter 5

Model Registry: Governance, Lineage, and Versioning

Behind every reliable production model lies a detailed record of its journey—from training and approvals to stage transitions and recovery. This chapter uncovers how MLflow's Model Registry transforms chaotic model sprawl into a governed, auditable, and collaborative process, empowering teams to track model lineage, enforce controls, and drive responsible ML operations at scale.

5.1. Model Registry API Usage

The Model Registry is a centralized repository for managing the lifecycle of machine learning models, bridging the gap between experimentation and deployment. MLflow provides comprehensive APIs that facilitate the registration, versioning, stage transitioning, and querying of models, enabling robust lifecycle management and promoting systematic development workflows.

Registering a model captures a specific iteration of an MLflow model artifact and makes it accessible for lifecycle management. This process involves creating a new registered model entry or adding a new version to an existing registered model.

A model is typically logged during an experiment run using `mlflow.pyfunc.log_model` or similar functions. Following this, the model artifact path and the run ID are used to create a new model version in the registry.

```
import mlflow
from mlflow.exceptions import MlflowException

model_name = "CustomerChurnModel"
run_id = "a1b2c3d4e5f6g7h8i9j0"
model_uri = f"runs:/{run_id}/model"

try:
    # Create a new registered model if it doesn't exist
    client = mlflow.tracking.MlflowClient()
    client.get_registered_model(model_name)
except MlflowException:
    client.create_registered_model(model_name)

# Create a new model version linking to the model artifact
model_version = client.create_model_version(
    name=model_name,
    source=model_uri,
    run_id=run_id
)
```

This approach ensures that the registered model is explicitly tracked, linking physical artifacts with their logical model identity within the registry.

Beyond creating versions, metadata such as descriptions, aliasing tags, or custom properties on registered models or specific versions can be updated. Precise metadata management is crucial for traceability and clarity across collaborative teams.

```
client.update_model_version(
    name=model_name,
    version=model_version.version,
    description="Improved feature engineering and hyperparameter
```

```
      tuning."
)
```

Similarly, descriptions for the registered model itself can be updated to maintain overall documentation quality.

MLflow Model Registry supports standard lifecycle stages: None (no stage), Staging, Production, and Archived. Transitioning a model version between these stages orchestrates its deployment status and governance workflow.

A systematic progression might involve moving a model from None to Staging for validation, and then to Production upon approval.

```
from mlflow.entities.model_registry import ModelVersionStatus

client.transition_model_version_stage(
    name=model_name,
    version=model_version.version,
    stage="Staging",
    archive_existing_versions=True  # Archive previous staging
      models
)
```

The optional argument archive_existing_versions ensures exclusivity at each stage, which is essential to avoid ambiguity in deployment.

Stages serve as authoritative signals for downstream deployment pipelines or inference servers to programmatically select the appropriate model version.

Efficient access to registry content is vital for operationalizing models. MLflow's APIs allow detailed querying of registered models, their versions, stages, and associated metadata, enabling dynamic model discovery and validation.

Listing all registered models:

```
registered_models = client.list_registered_models()
for rm in registered_models:
    print(f"Model: {rm.name}, Description: {rm.description}")
```

Retrieving all versions of a specific registered model:

```
versions = client.get_latest_versions(model_name, stages=["
    Production", "Staging"])
for v in versions:
    print(f"Version {v.version}: Stage={v.current_stage}, Created
        on {v.creation_timestamp}")
```

Filtering on stages simplifies selection for deployment or analysis. Additionally, querying specific versions by version number or filtering by tags and annotations is supported, offering fine-grained registry interrogation capabilities critical for automation.

Organizing models across stages enhances reproducibility, auditability, and deployment safety. Typical workflows adopt these conventions:

- **Development Stage (None)**: Early iterations and experimental models without explicit stage assignment.

- **Staging Stage**: Candidates that have passed initial validation tests and are under performance monitoring.

- **Production Stage**: Models approved for serving in real-time or batch inference pipelines.

- **Archived Stage**: Deprecated or superseded models retained for historical reference.

Automated workflows orchestrate transitions using CI/CD pipelines, invoking MLflow's APIs to advance models through their lifecycle based on quality gates defined by testing frameworks, bias assessments, or performance thresholds.

MLflow's web interface complements API interactions by offering intuitive workflows for registering models, updating descriptions, and transitioning stages interactively. The API calls under the hood sync with UI actions faithfully, making it possible to script complex automated pipelines or perform quick manual adjustments as needed.

For example, the manual promotion of a model through the UI mirrors the `transition_model_version_stage` function under the API, ensuring consistency regardless of interaction method.

Robust API usage requires consideration of potential conflicts or race conditions when multiple actors attempt simultaneous modifications. The MLflow client raises exceptions on invalid state transitions such as reusing an existing model name or moving a version to a stage that violates uniqueness constraints.

Implementing retries, optimistic concurrency control, and idempotency in automation scripts mitigates these conflicts:

```
import time

def safe_transition(client, name, version, stage, attempts=3):
    for _ in range(attempts):
        try:
            client.transition_model_version_stage(name, version,
        stage, archive_existing_versions=True)
            break
        except MlflowException as e:
            print(f"Transition failed: {e}, retrying...")
            time.sleep(2)
```

Such practices ensure stability in continuous integration and deployment environments where multiple teams or pipelines may interact with the registry concurrently.

The Model Registry API encapsulates the full lifecycle management ecosystem, enabling data scientists and operations teams to manage models with rigor and precision. Mastery of these mechanics establishes foundational control and traceability indispensable for industrial-scale machine learning deployments.

5.2. Automated Promotion and Approval Pipelines

Continuous Integration and Continuous Deployment (CI/CD) pipelines extend beyond code delivery into the realm of data science model lifecycle management, where automated promotion and approval mechanisms are critical for ensuring the integrity and reliability of models in production. Constructing automated pipelines that incorporate stage transitions, formal approvals, and promotions within a model registry enables seamless collaboration between data scientists, reviewers, and operations teams while embedding policy-driven governance into the release process.

Central to such pipelines is the notion of *stage promotion*, where models evolve through defined lifecycle states-commonly Staging, Production, and sometimes Archived. Rather than relying on manual updates or ad-hoc scripts, automating these state transitions guarantees reproducibility and auditability, providing clear traceability of model evolution. Automated promotion typically involves integrating CI/CD tools with the model registry, leveraging APIs to programmatically update model metadata, version status, and associated artifacts.

A foundational approach is to structure the pipeline as a series of well-defined jobs triggered by events such as model registration or successful completion of tests and validations. Each job performs specific checks-ranging from quality metrics verification and bias assessment to compliance scans-before forwarding the model to the next stage. This method reduces human error, enforces consistency, and accelerates iterative experimentation.

Approvals, often representing explicit gatekeeping actions by reviewers, are embedded into the pipeline using both manual intervention steps and automated policy evaluators. For manual approvals, modern CI/CD platforms support *approval gates* or *hold steps*, where an authorized stakeholder must validate the model readiness before continuation. These gates add accountability, incorporating human expertise into otherwise automated flows.

Conversely, policy-driven automation employs codified rules that automatically approve or reject models based on permit policies encoded as scripts or YAML configurations. For example, a policy may require that a model's area under the curve (AUC) exceeds a threshold and that fairness metrics comply with organizational standards. Any violation triggers automatic rejection or rollbacks, minimizing latency introduced by manual checks.

Integration with version control and artifact repositories further enhances automation fidelity. Embedding model lineage information-that is, linking models to source code commits, data versions, and environment configurations-facilitates comprehensive impact analysis. This lineage mapping aids approvers in contextualizing changes and verifying reproducibility. Pipelines can automatically retrieve associated metadata upon new model registration and incorporate it into dashboards or reports presented during approval phases.

Consider the case of a pipeline orchestrated by a tool such as Jenkins, GitLab CI, or GitHub Actions. After a data scientist pushes model training code and data triggers a pipeline run, the model is trained and registered in the model registry. The pipeline then initiates a validation stage where automated tests invoke regulatory compliance modules and bias detectors. Passing validation prompts an approval job, which either pauses for manual review or queries automated policy engines. Upon approval, an API call promotes the model to the Production stage, simultaneously triggering deployment workflows.

Implementing this flow requires precise scripting and configuration. Example pseudocode using a workflow definition language:

```
def train_and_register_model():
    model = train_model(data)
    model_version = register_model(model)
    return model_version

def validate_model(model_version):
    metrics = evaluate_model(model_version)
    if metrics['accuracy'] < ACCURACY_THRESHOLD:
        raise ValidationError("Accuracy below threshold")
    if not check_fairness(metrics):
        raise ValidationError("Fairness checks failed")
```

```
def approval_gate(model_version):
    if manual_approval_required:
        wait_for_manual_approval(model_version)
    else:
        policy_result = run_policy_engine(model_version)
        if not policy_result.approved:
            raise ApprovalError("Policy rejection")

def promote_model(model_version):
    update_registry_stage(model_version, "Production")
    trigger_deployment(model_version)

def pipeline():
    model_version = train_and_register_model()
    validate_model(model_version)
    approval_gate(model_version)
    promote_model(model_version)
```

The model registry API serves as the central integration point for the promotion commands. For instance, an HTTP PATCH request to update the model version's stage might look like:

```
curl -X PATCH "https://model-registry.company.com/api/models/{
    model_id}/versions/{version_id}" \
    -H "Authorization: Bearer $API_TOKEN" \
    -H "Content-Type: application/json" \
    -d '{"stage":"Production"}'
```

Systematic logging and audit trails accompany each stage transition and approval decision, ensuring that governance and compliance requirements are met. Audit records typically include timestamps, user identities for manual approvals, metric snapshots, and policy evaluation outcomes. This data forms the backbone for audits and postmortem analyses when production anomalies occur.

The orchestration of multi-role collaboration is a key benefit of automated pipelines. Data scientists can focus on experimentation without concern for manual staging procedures. Reviewers receive notifications and context-enriched dashboards for evaluation, with all requests tracked transparently. Operations teams gain confidence through policy-enforced promotions, reducing deployment risk. Additionally, rollback strategies can be automated as part of the pipeline, enabling swift reversion to prior stable model versions if issues surface post-deployment.

In complex environments, pipelines may integrate with external identity and access management (IAM) systems to enforce role-based access controls (RBAC) on promotion actions, restricting who can trigger or approve transitions. Coupled with policy engines, this integration establishes robust governance frameworks essential in regulated industries.

Automated promotion and approval pipelines materialize a policy-driven, collaborative framework that elevates model governance and operational excellence. By systematically embedding validation, controlled approvals, and stage transitions into CI/CD workflows interfaced with the model registry, organizations realize faster feedback loops, improved auditability, and reduced human error. The automation of these lifecycle phases is foundational to scaling trustworthy machine learning deployments in production environments.

5.3. Access Control and Permissions

Securing registry assets within modern AI model deployment environments necessitates a meticulous approach to access control and permission management. Role-Based Access Control (RBAC) stands as a cornerstone strategy for safeguarding sensitive model artifacts while facilitating seamless collaboration across diverse teams. RBAC establishes a structured framework where permissions are assigned to roles rather than to individual users, thereby simplifying management and enforcing the principle of least privilege.

At the core of RBAC are three primary components: *users*, *roles*, and *permissions*. Users represent the individual actors requiring access, roles encapsulate a collection of permissions that correspond to organizational functions or responsibilities, and permissions specify allowable actions on resources such as models, datasets, or registry metadata. By associating users with roles and assigning roles precise permissions, administrators can achieve granular control over who can perform operations such as model registration, updating, deletion, or promotion to production stages.

Effective implementation begins with a decomposition of required capabilities into modular permission sets. For example, typical registry actions can be grouped as follows:

- **Read**: Viewing model metadata, version history, or associated artifacts.

- **Write**: Uploading new model versions or updating metadata.

- **Manage**: Controlling lifecycle stages, including archiving or deleting models.

- **Administer**: Configuring access policies, defining roles, and managing user assignments.

This categorization enables organizations to map roles such as *Data Scientist, ML Engineer, Reviewer*, and *Administrator* to appropriate permission bundles. For instance, a Data Scientist may possess *Read* and *Write* permissions to develop and register models, whereas an Administrator holds *Administer* privileges encompassing full control.

The enforcement of such controls is often integrated within registry platforms using authorization engines that evaluate user credentials against role assignments at the time of each request. Tokens or certificates issued during authentication embed role claims, which the registry service uses to permit or deny actions atomically and without ambiguity. Ensuring that tokens have a limited lifetime, along with secure revocation mechanisms, adds an additional defensive layer against unauthorized access.

Cross-team collaboration is significantly enhanced by RBAC's flexibility in defining roles tailored to project needs. Interdisciplinary teams can share access to models with well-defined boundaries, allowing, for example, a DevOps team to manage deployment stages while restricting them from modifying underlying model weights or training parameters. Moreover, time-bound or conditional role assignments enable scenarios such as temporary elevated access during an incident or controlled experimentation phases, enforced through policy engines or integrating with Identity and Access Management (IAM) solutions.

Granular permissions extend beyond simple action-based controls by incorporating resource-level restrictions. Access can be limited to specific projects, namespaces, or even individual model versions. This fine-grained model ensures that sensitive artifacts-such as high-stakes production models or intellectual property-remain accessible only to authorized personnel. Implementing such scopes requires registries and authentication systems capable of processing hierarchical permission schemas and context-sensitive policies.

An important aspect in complex environments is auditability, which ensures that every access or modification attempt is logged comprehensively. Audit logs provide a forensic trail for compliance, security incident investigation, and internal governance. These logs typically record the identity of the actor, roles assumed, the action performed, target resources, timestamp, and outcome. Integration with centralized security information and event management (SIEM) tools is recommended to facilitate real-time monitoring and anomaly detection.

From a practical standpoint, consider an example using a declarative RBAC policy modeled as JSON or YAML within a registry access control system:

```
{
  "roles": {
    "data_scientist": {
```

```
      "permissions": ["model:read", "model:write"]
    },
    "ml_engineer": {
      "permissions": ["model:read", "model:write", "model:manage
      "]
    },
    "auditor": {
      "permissions": ["model:read"]
    },
    "admin": {
      "permissions": ["*"]
    }
  },
  "users": {
    "alice": ["data_scientist"],
    "bob": ["ml_engineer"],
    "carol": ["auditor"],
    "dave": ["admin"]
  }
}
```

Here, user `alice` is confined to read and write capabilities, enabling model development without the ability to manage lifecycle stages. User `dave`, with the admin role, has unrestricted access. This model supports clear demarcation of duties and reduces attack surfaces arising from unnecessary privileges.

For environments requiring dynamic adjustment of permissions, policy-as-code frameworks can automate the propagation of access changes based on organizational workflows. Tools such as Open Policy Agent (OPA) facilitate the creation of declarative policies evaluated at runtime, allowing for expressive constraints such as time-based access, IP-based restrictions, or multi-factor authenticated actions.

The amalgamation of RBAC with granular permissions and policy enforcement mechanisms constitutes a robust methodology for securing model registry assets. This approach harmonizes stringent access restrictions with flexible collaboration capabilities, enabling organizations to maintain control while accelerating innovation through shared, secure model development lifecycle management.

5.4. Lineage, Provenance, and Auditing

Machine learning operations demand rigorous traceability to ensure models can be reliably reproduced, validated, and audited across their lifecycle. MLflow, as a versatile platform for managing machine learning workflows, emphasizes comprehensive lineage tracking, linking model versions explicitly to the underlying code, data, and experiments that produced them. This lineage serves as an immutable audit trail, providing critical transparency required for establishing trust, satisfying regulatory compliance, and facilitating debugging in complex machine learning systems.

At its core, MLflow enables capturing and querying the complete provenance of any model by associating it with the full context of its creation. This includes the exact versions of datasets, the executable code (often as source files, notebooks, or containerized environments), parameter configurations, and even hardware or software environment details. Every artifact generated within MLflow—including models, runs, metrics, and parameters—contains metadata references explicitly linking these components. For instance, a model version saved via MLflow Model Registry retains information about its corresponding MLflow run, which is in turn associated with the source code commit identifier, input data sources, and other experimental variables.

This lineage is materialized through MLflow's tracking API and registry. During experimentation, users log parameters, metrics, models, and tags to uniquely identify the run and its context. Consider the process represented by the following example code snippet that logs a model along with pertinent provenance metadata:

```
import mlflow
import mlflow.sklearn

with mlflow.start_run() as run:
    # Log parameters and metrics
    mlflow.log_param("alpha", 0.5)
    mlflow.log_metric("rmse", 3.45)
```

```
# Train and log model artifact
model = train_model(data, alpha=0.5)
mlflow.sklearn.log_model(model, "model")

# Log source code version (e.g., git commit)
mlflow.set_tag("git_commit", "a1b2c3d4e5f6")

# Log data version or fingerprint
mlflow.set_tag("training_data_hash", "9f86d081884c7d65")

# Get run id to link with model version
run_id = run.info.run_id
```

This provenance metadata illustrates key traceability points: the hyperparameters (alpha), the evaluation metric (rmse), and the unique identifiers for the exact source code revision (git_commit) and dataset version (training_data_hash). Together, these elements form a cohesive lineage record that can be queried later to understand precisely which inputs generated the deployed model.

When this model is subsequently registered in the MLflow Model Registry, the linkage to its originating run's metadata is preserved. A model version's detailed history includes timestamps, user actions, stage transitions (e.g., from Staging to Production), and explicitly references the source run ID. The Model Registry provides a centralized mechanism to visualize and audit lineage relationships, displaying dependencies between different model versions and their respective experiments.

The importance of such lineage extends beyond operational management into domains demanding stringent governance and compliance. Auditable trails enable organizations to demonstrate accountability by revealing how each model decision correlates with reproducible data and code artifacts. Regulatory frameworks such as GDPR or FDA guidelines for software as a medical device increasingly expect demonstrable reproducibility and explainability for automated decision-making systems. Lineage tracking via MLflow provides proof that models were built from vetted datasets and validated software, preventing hidden biases or unauthorized modifications from compromising outcomes.

From a debugging perspective, tracing issues in production models benefits immensely from complete lineage data. Suppose an unexpected production anomaly appears—for example, degraded prediction accuracy or bias detected in audit monitoring. Being able to traverse the lineage graph enables practitioners to pinpoint the exact model version, training dataset, or source code iteration responsible. This drastically reduces root cause analysis time by avoiding guesswork and blind searches through multiple disconnected artifacts.

Furthermore, lineage data supports continuous integration and deployment (CI/CD) pipelines for machine learning, often dubbed MLOps. Automated workflows can leverage MLflow's lineage information to enforce quality gates, validating that only models whose associated data and code fulfill set standards are promoted to production. This ensures that models undergo thorough peer review and testing before impacting live systems.

Underneath the high-level abstractions, MLflow's implementation of lineage uses a flexible metadata store, commonly backed by relational databases, that indexes entities such as experiments, runs, artifacts, parameters, metrics, and tags. These entities are linked by unique identifiers and relational references, enabling efficient retrieval of lineage graphs. Users may navigate from a model version backward to the experiment run, then further back to source data and code metadata, forming a complete provenance chain.

In summary, the linkage MLflow establishes between model versions, code revisions, data snapshots, and experimental contexts creates a comprehensive and transparent audit trail. This lineage capability is essential for instilling confidence in machine learning systems by ensuring they are reproducible, verifiable, and auditable. It supports operational robustness through debugging and model governance while fulfilling regulatory and ethical mandates that demand provenance awareness. Robust lineage thus forms a foundational pillar upon which trustworthy and maintainable machine learning deployments are constructed.

5.5. Rollback and Recovery Procedures

In dynamic production environments where model registries serve as the backbone for deploying and managing machine learning artifacts, the ability to effectuate rollback and recovery is paramount. These procedures ensure business continuity by minimizing operational risk and maintaining system integrity amidst inevitable errors, misconfigurations, or system failures. This section explores pragmatic strategies for undoing staged changes, reinstating prior model versions, and designing comprehensive disaster recovery plans within the model registry framework.

Modern model registries provide explicit versioning and stage management mechanisms, such as Staging, Production, Archived, and Deleted states. Undoing changes at the staging level entails precise control to revert models to prior states without disrupting ongoing workflows. This typically involves atomic transitions managed through transactional metadata updates to the registry's underlying data store. A straightforward approach to rollback in this context is the reversion of a model's stage attribute to its preceding state accompanied by metadata annotations recording who performed the rollback and why. For example, if a model's promotion to Production resulted in degradation of service, one can revert it by reassigning the latest stable checkpoint's version to the Production stage.

The rollback process often leverages capabilities such as:

- **Model Version Pinning**: Locking a tested and approved version in a particular stage to prevent inadvertent overwrites.

- **Immutable Version Snapshotting**: Ensuring model artifacts and metadata associated with each version are stored immutably, enabling exact restoration at any required point.

- **Audit Trails**: Maintaining detailed logs of state transitions, metadata changes, and user actions to facilitate forensic analysis and rollback verification.

An exemplar command sequence in a CLI-oriented model registry environment to rollback to a previous stable version might appear as follows:

```
# List model versions with stages and timestamps
model-registry list-versions --model my-ml-model

# Set model version 12 back to Production stage
model-registry transition-stage --model my-ml-model --version 12
    --stage Production

# Archive unstable version 13 to prevent its usage
model-registry transition-stage --model my-ml-model --version 13
    --stage Archived
```

The critical consideration here is transactionality and consistency; the registry must enforce that only one version holds the Production stage at a time. Advanced registries support conditional transitions or staged rollout policies to automate safe rollback.

Restoring previous model versions extends beyond mere stage reassignment. Since models often depend on code, configuration, and environment specifications, a holistic restoration requires reconstituting the entire serving ecosystem to the previous known-good state. This includes:

- **Artifact Recovery**: Fetching model binaries, serialized objects, or container images from artifact stores or object repositories aligned with the previous version.

- **Environment Reconstruction**: Reinstating dependencies and runtime environments, often using version-controlled environment manifests such as Dockerfiles or Conda environments.

- **Configuration Syncing**: Adjusting serving configurations, feature store pointers, and data pipeline integrations to align with the restored model version.

These actions are vital to avoid semantic drift caused by mismatched model-environment combinations, which impair inference correctness. Automated pipelines that integrate model registry metadata with infrastructure-as-code (IaC) templates enable seamless rollback at both model and serving stack levels.

Disaster recovery planning within the model registry context encompasses robust data protection, rapid restoration, and continuous availability. Key elements of a resilient disaster recovery strategy include:

Regular Backup and Replication

Model registry metadata, model artifacts, and related configurations should be regularly backed up to geographically distributed and durable storage media. Versioned backups ensure point-in-time recovery and protection against accidental deletions or data corruption. Synchronous or asynchronous replication to failover clusters mitigates single points of failure.

Failover Automation and Orchestration

Recovery processes must be codified and automated to enable minimal human intervention during outages. Orchestration frameworks employing well-defined runbooks can trigger failover by promoting secondary registry instances or restoring from backups systematically, including consistency checks.

Validation and Readiness Testing

Periodic validation of rollback and recovery operations is essential to guarantee that procedures work in realistic scenarios. This testing includes:

- Simulated failures and restoration drills.

- Verification of model consistency post-rollback.

- Monitoring of system performance and error rates after recovery.

Change Management and Governance

Robust governance enforces policies such as mandatory approvals before stage transitions, access controls for rollback permissions, and ensuring audit compliance. Role-based access minimizes accidental or malicious rollback operations that could destabilize production.

Implementing these strategies effectively requires tight integration between the model registry, continuous integration and deployment (CI/CD) pipelines, and infrastructure management platforms. By embedding rollback and recovery logic into automated workflows, teams can achieve rapid remediation with reduced operational overhead, ultimately enhancing system reliability.

Failure to plan and execute these procedures can result in prolonged downtime, degraded service levels, and loss of user trust. Consequently, rollback and recovery procedures represent a cornerstone capability for organizations managing machine learning lifecycles at scale, underpinning resilient and adaptive production environments.

5.6. Model Governance in Regulated Environments

In highly regulated industries, such as healthcare, finance, and aerospace, the deployment and management of machine learning models demand stringent governance frameworks to ensure compliance with legal, ethical, and operational standards. MLflow's Model Registry provides a structured platform for model lifecycle management, but its adoption in regulated environments requires an understanding of the intersection between technical capabilities and regulatory mandates. This section examines policy, documentation, and compliance requirements integral to using MLflow's Registry, and outlines best practices to uphold governance rigor.

Regulated organizations must establish comprehensive policies that embed the use of MLflow's Registry within a broader governance strategy. Policies should address model version control, access management, auditability, and change management. A fundamental requirement is the definition of roles and responsibilities for stakeholders involved in the model lifecycle, including data scientists, compliance officers, and IT administrators.

Explicit policy mandates should stipulate how models are registered, promoted across stages (e.g., "Staging", "Production"), and archived. For example, model promotion workflows must incorporate approval gates where automated tests, performance benchmarks, and fairness assessments are reviewed. MLflow's capabilities for stage transitions facilitate this, but organizational policy must specify the criteria and the approval process to enforce discipline and traceability.

Policies must also articulate retention periods for model artifacts and audit logs, aligned with legal requirements such as GDPR, HIPAA, or the SEC's Regulation SCI. MLflow facilitates the storage of model metadata including creator identity, creation timestamps, and source code references, which are foundational for meeting these regulatory demands.

Comprehensive documentation is a cornerstone of model governance in regulated environments. MLflow's Registry supports automated metadata capture, but it is imperative to augment this with standardized documentation templates capturing the rationale, data lineage, validation results, and intended use cases of each model version.

Documentation should include, but not be limited to, the following elements:

- **Model Description and Purpose:** Clear articulation of the model's objective, assumptions, and business context.

- **Data Provenance:** Detailed lineage of training data, including source systems, preprocessing steps, and data quality checks.

- **Validation Artifacts:** Results from model performance metrics, bias and fairness assessments, and robustness testing.

- **Approval Records:** Evidence of review and sign-off by relevant stakeholders at each lifecycle stage, captured either within MLflow or integrated tools.

Because MLflow's Registry allows attaching custom tags and notes, organizations can institute fields for compliance-critical annotations. Maintaining such structured documentation not only supports compliance audits but also strengthens internal audit capabilities and continuous improvement cycles.

Compliance in regulated sectors requires embedding controls and checkpoints into the model management workflow. MLflow's Registry can be integrated with external governance systems such as enterprise identity management, automated testing frameworks, and regulatory reporting tools, creating a cohesive compliance ecosystem.

Access controls must be rigorously enforced, leveraging authentication and authorization mechanisms that restrict who can register, modify, or promote models. Integration with single sign-on (SSO) and role-based access control (RBAC) tools ensures that only authorized personnel interact with model assets. MLflow supports these through API-level authentication hooks and can be deployed behind secure infrastructure gateways.

131

Change management protocols are critical; MLflow's versioning of models inherently supports traceability of changes, but organizations must extend this to include pre-deployment validation checklists and rollback mechanisms. Incorporating automated validation pipelines triggered on model registration or stage transition ensures that no model advances without satisfying governance criteria.

Audit readiness also hinges on logging and monitoring. MLflow records lifecycle events and metadata, but to fulfill stringent regulatory requirements, organizations must retain logs for required durations and provide mechanisms for immutable record-keeping. Combining MLflow with append-only storage systems or blockchain-inspired ledgers can provide tamper-evident audit trails.

- **Define Clear Governance Policies:** Develop detailed policies that integrate MLflow functionality with organizational compliance requirements, including model promotion criteria and retention rules.

- **Standardize Documentation:** Use MLflow's tagging and artifact storage features to embed comprehensive metadata and structured documentation throughout the model lifecycle.

- **Integrate with Access Management Systems:** Employ robust identity and role controls to ensure only authorized users perform key operations within the MLflow Registry.

- **Automate Validation and Testing:** Establish automated pipelines tied to MLflow's stage transitions that verify model quality, bias mitigation, and security compliance before approval.

- **Implement Immutable Audit Trails:** Leverage MLflow's logging with supplementary secure storage to create tamper-resistant records for audit and compliance review.

- **Enforce Lifecycle Discipline:** Prohibit ad-hoc deployments by mandating that models can only be promoted through curated, policy-driven workflows managed in MLflow.

While MLflow streamlines many aspects of model lifecycle management, regulated industries face specific challenges when integrating this technology:

- **Regulatory Variability:** Different jurisdictions impose varying documentation standards and data privacy rules; MLflow's open design necessitates customizing implementations to meet these diverse requirements.

- **Cross-Functional Coordination:** Effective governance requires collaboration among data science, compliance, IT, and legal teams, posing operational challenges that extend beyond tool capabilities.

- **Technological Integration:** Seamlessly integrating MLflow with existing Enterprise Risk Management (ERM) and Governance, Risk, and Compliance (GRC) platforms demands careful architecture and investment.

Despite these challenges, the structured, metadata-rich environment enabled by MLflow's Model Registry serves as a foundation upon which robust governance frameworks can be constructed, ensuring machine learning workflows align with the highest standards of regulatory compliance and ethical responsibility.

Chapter 6

Advanced Experimentation, Automation, and Pipeline Integration

Push the boundaries of ML experimentation with robust automation, reproducible pipelines, and seamless orchestration. This chapter reveals how to scale and automate ML with MLflow—connecting experiments to continuous retraining, multi-stage deployments, and hybrid cloud workflows. Discover how to transform your ML infrastructure from a patchwork of scripts into a coherent, production-grade system capable of rapid iteration and resilient operation.

6.1. Designing Reproducible ML Pipelines

Reproducibility in machine learning (ML) pipelines is essential for validating models, debugging, ensuring compliance, and maintaining systems over the long term. Achieving end-to-end reproducibility requires a systematic approach encompassing all stages: data ingestion, preprocessing, model training, evaluation, and deployment. The design of ML pipelines must emphasize modularity, traceability, and automation, ensuring that each step can be repeated exactly, even in complex environments involving multiple data sources and transformations.

Modular Design Patterns

A reproducible ML pipeline begins with modular design. Each pipeline component-data collection, feature engineering, model training, and deployment-should be encapsulated in discrete, well-defined modules with clear interfaces. This separation allows for independent development, testing, and versioning of components.

Modules typically implement the following design patterns:

- **Immutable data inputs and outputs:** Each stage receives input artifacts (e.g., datasets, model parameters) and produces output artifacts without side effects. Immutability ensures that rerunning a module with the same input will always yield the same output.

- **Parameterization and configuration management:** Pipelines should externalize hyperparameters, paths, and environment settings to facilitate consistent execution across different runs and environments.

- **Idempotency:** Running any module multiple times with identical inputs and parameters should not alter the pipeline state or results. This property simplifies error recovery and rerun strategies.

Building on these patterns, pipeline frameworks such as Apache Airflow, Kubeflow Pipelines, or MLflow Projects encourage a composable design where each operator or step can be independently versioned and containerized. This containerization isolates dependencies and execution contexts, further strengthening reproducibility.

Template Workflows for Consistency

Template workflows codify a standard sequence of steps and best practices to minimize variation between runs or across teams. A typical ML pipeline template incorporates:

1. **Data ingestion:** Automated extraction from raw sources, accompanied by checksum validation and timestamping to detect changes or data drift.

2. **Data validation and preprocessing:** Schema enforcement, outlier detection, and transformation steps tracked via metadata to guarantee consistent data state.

3. **Feature engineering:** Deterministic feature calculations, stored alongside versioned code, preferably as serialized artifacts or feature stores.

4. **Model training and tuning:** Fixed random seeds and well-documented hyperparameter search spaces ensure reproducible model fitting.

5. **Evaluation and validation:** Standardized metrics computed on isolated test sets, with results logged to trace experiment lineage.

6. **Deployment and monitoring:** Automated packaging, version-controlled deployment manifests, and real-time monitoring of model performance and data drift.

Such templates function as blueprints that enforce reproducibility through automation and reduce human error. Utilizing workflow orchestration tools enables scheduling, retries, and clear dependency graphs that transparently communicate the pipeline's execution logic.

Strategies for Tracking and Repeatability

Maintaining reproducibility extends beyond initial design to runtime tracking. The following strategies are critical:

- **Data versioning:** Employ tools like Data Version Control (DVC) or built-in platform solutions to snapshot datasets and preprocessing outputs. Data hashing and immutable storage guarantee access to historic input states.

- **Code version control:** Tie pipeline executions to specific Git commits or tagged releases. This linkage allows exact code retrieval corresponding to any run.

- **Experiment tracking:** Record all parameters, hyperparameters, environment variables, and hardware configurations used during training. Tools such as MLflow Tracking or Weights & Biases facilitate this process with automatic logging.

- **Containerization and environment reproducibility:** Use deterministic container builds (e.g., Docker with pinned dependencies) or managed environments to prevent drift in software libraries or system dependencies.

- **Artifact management:** Persist intermediate outputs, models, and evaluation results with unique identifiers and metadata. Centralized artifact stores provide audit trails and enable rollback or re-deployment.

- **Immutable logs and audit trails:** Capture detailed logs of data ingestion times, transformation parameters, pipeline execution timing, and error events. Immutable log storage supports regulatory requirements and debugging.

138

Practical implementation example

A reproducible pipeline might be scripted as follows using a declarative pipeline definition and experiment tracking with MLflow:

```
import mlflow
import mlflow.sklearn
from sklearn.ensemble import RandomForestClassifier

def train_model(train_data, params, run_name="rf_train"):
    with mlflow.start_run(run_name=run_name):
        mlflow.log_params(params)
        X_train, y_train = train_data
        model = RandomForestClassifier(**params, random_state=42)
        model.fit(X_train, y_train)
        mlflow.sklearn.log_model(model, "model")
        preds = model.predict(X_train)
        accuracy = (preds == y_train).mean()
        mlflow.log_metric("training_accuracy", accuracy)
        return model
```

This example demonstrates key principles: parameter logging, fixed random seed for reproducibility, and artifact logging. By enforcing such patterns across all pipeline steps, the entire workflow becomes auditable and repeatable.

Summary of design considerations

Implementing reproducible ML pipelines requires a holistic approach that spans design, automation, and monitoring. Core principles include:

- Designing modular, immutable components with explicit inputs and outputs.

- Employing templated workflows to enforce consistent sequences of tasks.

- Leveraging tools for version control of data, code, and environments.

- Capturing comprehensive metadata, logs, and artifacts throughout pipeline execution.

These practices collectively empower practitioners to rerun experiments under identical conditions and confidently promote models to production knowing that the entire lifecycle is documented and repeatable.

6.2. Orchestrating End-to-End ML Workflows

Modern machine learning systems extend beyond standalone model development into complex pipelines that integrate diverse data sources, transformation steps, model training, evaluation, deployment, and monitoring. Coordinating these stages reliably and efficiently requires robust orchestration frameworks. Widely adopted tools such as Apache Airflow, Prefect, and Dagster provide comprehensive platforms to design, schedule, and maintain workflows while managing intricate dependencies intrinsic to end-to-end ML pipelines.

At the foundation of ML workflow orchestration lies the directed acyclic graph (DAG) abstraction, where tasks represent discrete units of work—data extraction, feature engineering, model training, validation, or deployment steps—and edges encode their execution dependencies. This graph structure enables orchestration tools to analyze task precedence and optimize scheduling, guaranteeing correct execution order under failure or rerun scenarios.

Apache Airflow, one of the earliest and most popular orchestrators, excels with its declarative Python-based DAG definition and scheduling capabilities. Tasks in Airflow are encapsulated as Python callable operators or externally managed jobs. The scheduler triggers task runs based on time or event-driven schedules, while the metadata database tracks task state and runtime information. Airflow's extensibility and vast ecosystem facilitate integration with cloud storage, databases, containerized environments, and ML platforms, supporting pipeline components such as Spark jobs or TensorFlow training scripts.

To illustrate, a simplified Airflow DAG defining a daily ML training pipeline might use operators for data ingestion, feature processing, model fitting, and validation:

```
from airflow import DAG
from airflow.operators.python import PythonOperator
from datetime import datetime

def ingest_data():
    # Load and cache daily raw data
    pass

def process_features():
    # Generate features and store in feature store
    pass

def train_model():
    # Train model and save artifacts
    pass

def validate_model():
    # Evaluate model performance on test set
    pass

with DAG('ml_training_pipeline', start_date=datetime(2024, 1, 1),
        schedule_interval='@daily') as dag:
    ingest = PythonOperator(task_id='ingest_data',
    python_callable=ingest_data)
    features = PythonOperator(task_id='process_features',
    python_callable=process_features)
    train = PythonOperator(task_id='train_model', python_callable
    =train_model)
    validate = PythonOperator(task_id='validate_model',
    python_callable=validate_model)

    ingest >> features >> train >> validate
```

Prefect advances ML workflow orchestration by offering a hybrid model combining imperative and declarative paradigms, with a focus on ease of development and fault-tolerant execution. Unlike Airflow, Prefect enforces stateful task management internally and enables dynamic workflows adapted at runtime depending on live conditions. Its flow framework provides powerful APIs to orchestrate parallel and iterative computations, a crucial factor for hyperparameter optimization or retraining iterations. Prefect's native data passing mechanisms through task inputs and outputs reduce boilerplate and facilitate lineage tracking.

Dagster emphasizes type safety and strong development-time guarantees using typed inputs and outputs on pipeline solids (tasks) for ML workflows. It integrates natively with data catalogs and supports asset materialization, promoting modular pipeline development where each component's input-output interface is explicitly specified. This design improves observability and facilitates incremental re-execution, enabling only the downstream tasks to rerun when upstream data changes, which is vital for efficient iterative experimentation.

Scheduling complex dependencies involves managing conditional and parallel executions, branchings based on model metrics, or retries in response to transient failures. For example, a pipeline might conditionally trigger model deployment only if validation accuracy exceeds a threshold, or perform automated rollback otherwise. Technically, the orchestrator must support branching constructs or predicate-based task triggers implemented as dynamically evaluated sensors or hooks. Prefect supports this smoothly via Python control flow embedded in flows, while Airflow implements branching with the `BranchPythonOperator`.

Maintaining pipeline health in production requires continuous monitoring and alerting on task execution metrics such as success rate, duration, and resource consumption. Integrations with observability systems (e.g., Prometheus, Grafana, Datadog) enable real-time dashboards and SLA enforcement. Additionally, workflows must be resilient against task failures, implementing mechanisms like task retries, exponential backoff, and alert notifications for manual intervention. Modern orchestrators incorporate these features inherently, allowing ML engineers to specify retry logic and failure policies declaratively.

Automating iterative experiments, which involve multiple training runs with variant hyperparameters or data partitions, is facilitated by orchestrators supporting parameterized workflows and dynamic mapping constructs. For example, Prefect's mapped tasks execute a function over a collection of parameters in parallel, thereby automating grid or random hyperparameter searches without manual duplication of pipeline definitions. This automation reduces human error and accelerates ML experimentation cadence.

The seamless integration of ML workflow components with the orchestration backend depends on containerization and environment management. Airflow, Prefect, and Dagster all support container operators or Kubernetes executors, enabling isolation, reproducibility, and scalable execution across heterogeneous compute environments. This capability simplifies deploying workflows reliably across local, cloud, or hybrid infrastructures.

Orchestrating end-to-end ML workflows leverages the inherent DAG structure to ensure order and dependency management, combines conditional logic and parallelism for complex pipelines, and embeds monitoring and failure handling to maintain robustness. Tools like Airflow, Prefect, and Dagster provide complementary abstractions and capabilities to automate these processes, enabling ML teams to focus on modeling innovation rather than pipeline plumbing. The careful selection and adaptation of orchestration frameworks to specific ML project requirements fundamentally enhance operational efficiency, experiment management, and production reliability.

6.3. Continuous Training and Automated Retraining

Machine learning models are inherently susceptible to changes in data distribution, operational environments, and emerging domain requirements. Continuous training and automated retraining form critical processes that maintain and enhance the relevance, accuracy, and robustness of models post-deployment. Addressing phenomena such as data drift, performance degradation, and the arrival of new data is essential for ensuring long-term model efficacy and operational accountability.

Data drift, including covariate shift, prior probability shift, and concept drift, causes discrepancies between the training data distribution and the production data over time. Covariate shift denotes changes in the input feature distribution $P(X)$, while the conditional distribution $P(Y|X)$ remains stable. Concept drift, a more profound challenge, occurs when the relationship $P(Y|X)$ itself changes. Automated retraining strategies must detect and adapt to these shifts dynamically to prevent model obsolescence.

Automated retraining systems typically begin with robust monitoring frameworks that continuously evaluate model predictions and underlying data streams. Key performance indicators (KPIs) such as accuracy, precision, recall, F1-score, calibration metrics, and business-specific objectives must be tracked alongside statistical tests for data distribution changes such as the Kolmogorov-Smirnov test, Population Stability Index (PSI), and Wasserstein distance. Triggering conditions for retraining can be defined via threshold-based rules or learned anomaly detection models operating on these metrics.

A fundamental approach to automating retraining involves establishing feedback loops that capture new labeled data, model performance outcomes, and contextual metadata. The figure illustrates a typical continuous training architecture integrating data ingestion, model monitoring, retraining orchestration, and deployment pipelines.

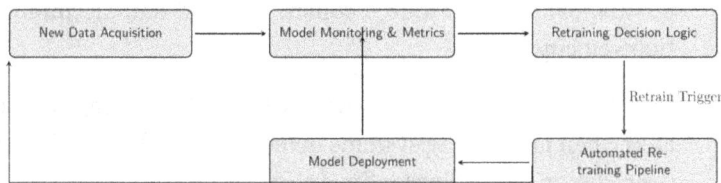

Retraining pipelines are often implemented using workflow management tools that enable modular, repeatable, and scalable executions. These pipelines encompass data preprocessing, feature engineering, model training, validation, and artifact management. Notably, they must ensure reproducibility by versioning datasets, model code, and hyperparameters. Integration with model governance frameworks is critical to maintain audit trails and compliance.

One effective technique for model adaptation is incremental learning, where models update their parameters continuously or periodically with newly acquired data instead of retraining from scratch. Algorithms such as online gradient descent, adaptive boosting variants, and streaming random forests support this paradigm. However, practitioners must balance incremental updates against risks of catastrophic forgetting and model drift amplification.

Another advanced strategy employs meta-learning or continual learning approaches to adapt the model's learning dynamics in response to changing distributions. Techniques such as elastic weight consolidation or memory-augmented networks can preserve previously acquired knowledge while incorporating new patterns efficiently.

When fresh labeled data arrives, retraining strategies can be categorized into scheduled retraining, performance-triggered retraining, and hybrid approaches:

- **Scheduled Retraining:** Models are retrained at fixed intervals, balancing resource constraints and data accumulation velocity.

- **Performance-Triggered Retraining:** Retraining is initiated when monitoring systems detect statistically significant degradation beyond predefined thresholds.

- **Hybrid Approaches:** Combine scheduled evaluations with performance-based triggers for greater flexibility.

Automated retraining workflows are often codified as algorithms embedded within DevOps and MLOps frameworks. Consider the pseudocode below, illustrating a simplified retraining trigger mechanism driven by performance monitoring:

```
def should_retrain(current_metric, baseline_metric, threshold
    =0.05):
    degradation = (baseline_metric - current_metric) /
    baseline_metric
    if degradation > threshold:
        return True
    return False

def retraining_loop():
    baseline_metric = evaluate_model()
    while True:
        current_metric = evaluate_model()
        if should_retrain(current_metric, baseline_metric):
            retrain_model()
            baseline_metric = current_metric
        sleep(monitoring_interval)
```

```
Output example:
Baseline accuracy: 0.92
Current accuracy: 0.88
Retrain triggered due to accuracy degradation of 4.3%
Model retrained.
New baseline accuracy: 0.91
```

Beyond accuracy metrics, incorporating holistic evaluation metrics such as fairness, robustness under adversarial scenarios, and resource utilization is critical during retraining decisions. Moreover, labeling latency and data annotation costs must be carefully managed, especially in scenarios where manual labeling is

involved. Semi-supervised learning and active learning can mitigate these challenges by prioritizing informative samples for annotation.

To ensure ongoing accountability and traceability, retraining processes must generate detailed logs and produce model cards summarizing training data versions, model architectures, hyperparameters, performance metrics, and deployment timestamps. These
records support reproducibility, compliance audits, and stakeholder communication.

Continuous training and automated retraining comprise a robust
system of proactive model management, leveraging monitoring,
feedback loops, adaptive algorithms, and orchestration pipelines.
Mastery of these techniques empowers organizations to sustain
machine learning efficacy amidst ever-evolving data landscapes,
ensuring models remain accurate, adaptive, and accountable
throughout their operational lifecycle.

6.4. Pipeline Versioning and Multi-Stage Deployments

In complex machine learning (ML) ecosystems, treating an ML
pipeline as an immutable artifact is paramount to ensuring reproducibility, maintainability, and operational safety. Unlike isolated model versioning, pipeline versioning encompasses the holistic workflow—data ingestion, feature engineering, model training, evaluation, and deployment—alongside all associated dependencies and configurations. This expanded scope demands rigorous strategies for organizing, versioning, promoting, and rolling
back entire pipelines, thus enabling robust multi-stage rollout processes.

Organizing Complete ML Pipelines

Structuring an ML pipeline begins with defining modular, composable components with explicit interfaces and clear inputs and out-puts. Each step—whether data preprocessing, feature extraction, or model training—is encapsulated as an independent, versioned unit. These components are then orchestrated by workflow managers or pipelines-as-code frameworks, enabling execution graphs that capture dependencies and parallelism.

Versioning pipelines effectively necessitates capturing not only the logical sequence of these components but also their specific versions and configuration parameters. This can be achieved by treating the pipeline definition as a configuration artifact stored in a version control system (VCS), where each commit corresponds to a distinct pipeline version. Within this definition, every component reference includes a version or hash tag to fix the exact code and environment state, guarding against drift due to upstream updates.

Pipeline Version Control and Dependency Management

While models are often tracked via model registries, pipeline version control integrates across multiple artifact repositories and dependency managers. Managing heterogeneous artifact types—code, data schemas, feature stores, and models—requires a unified metadata layer that binds them into coherent pipeline versions. This layer maintains lineage graphs that trace data origins, transformations, and model derivations with fine granularity.

For example, an ML pipeline version might reference:

- Data snapshot identifiers (e.g., dataset commit hashes or versioned tables)

- Feature engineering code versions and feature catalog metadata

- Model artifact versions from the model registry

- Container or environment image tags, including library dependencies and runtime configurations

To ensure deterministic pipeline executions, dependency management tools such as Conda, Docker, or specialized ML environment managers are integrated, encapsulating runtime environments in portable, reproducible containers. This end-to-end versioning composes a pipeline snapshot that can be reliably materialized, enabling auditability and deterministic reruns.

Multi-Stage Deployments: Canary, Staging, and Production

Pipeline promotion through a multi-stage deployment strategy mitigates risks inherent to ML lifecycle operations. This approach models deployment as a sequence of controlled stages, typically:

- **Development:** Initial pipeline testing and iterative improvements in isolated environments.

- **Staging:** Pre-production environment mirroring production settings for final validation, performance benchmarking, and integration tests.

- **Canary (or Shadow):** Limited production exposure where pipeline outputs are evaluated under real traffic conditions against the incumbent.

- **Production:** Full rollout after verifying stability, accuracy, and system metrics.

Promoting a pipeline version from staging to canary involves updating routing and inference services to divert a controlled traffic fraction to the new pipeline instance. Observability tools collect detailed performance and quality metrics, enabling quantitative comparisons with the production baseline. Transition decisions rely on automated gating criterions or manual reviews, accounting for latency, throughput, prediction accuracy, and business-specific KPIs.

Rollback Strategies and Safety Mechanisms

Despite rigorous validation, unforeseen issues may surface post-deployment. Well-defined rollback mechanisms are critical to rapidly restore a stable state. In pipeline versioning, rollbacks entail:

- Reverting workflow orchestrators to execute previous pipeline versions, ensuring all dependencies (models, data, code, environment) are consistent with the rollback target.

- Restoring inference routing configurations to redirect traffic back to the last known good deployment.

- Reprocessing any necessary downstream data or predictions if rollback affects batch or streaming inference results.

Rollback control can be automated through policy-driven frameworks integrated with continuous delivery pipelines, allowing quick reversion on error detection or performance degradation. Maintaining immutable, versioned artifacts and environments simplifies rollback by reducing configuration drift and incompatibility risks.

Traceability and Auditability

Complete pipeline versioning supports extensive traceability, central to compliance, debugging, and continuous improvement. The lineage graph not only identifies all pipeline artifacts used in each production run but also documents execution metadata, parameter settings, and evaluation results. Such detailed audit trails enable retrospective analysis of prediction behavior, error root causes, or data drift phenomena.

Furthermore, advanced metadata stores implement searchable registries where pipeline versions are indexed by attributes such as feature versions, dataset snapshots, model hyperparameters, or deployment timestamps. Integration with monitoring and alerting systems creates feedback loops that inform subsequent pipeline iterations, closing the ML lifecycle loop with continuous validation and deployment governance.

Illustrative Example: Pipeline Promotion and Rollback Workflow

Consider the following algorithmic representation of multi-stage pipeline promotion within a deployment orchestration system:

Algorithm 1 Multi-Stage Pipeline Promotion and Rollback

1: **procedure** PromotePipeline($currentVersion, targetStage$)
2:     $candidate \leftarrow$ RetrievePipelineVersion($currentVersion$)
3:     ValidatePipeline($candidate$)
4:     **if** $targetStage =$ Canary **then**
5:         RouteTrafficFraction($candidate$, fraction=0.1)
6:         MonitorMetrics($candidate$)
7:         **if** MetricsSatisfactory($candidate$) **then**
8:             PromotePipeline($candidate$, Production)
9:         **else**
10:            RollbackPipeline($currentVersion$)
11:         **end if**
12:     **else if** $targetStage =$ Production **then**
13:         RouteTrafficAll($candidate$)
14:         RetirePreviousVersion($currentVersion$)
15:     **else**
16:         DeployToStageEnvironment($candidate, targetStage$)
17:     **end if**
18: **end procedure**
19: **procedure** RollbackPipeline($previousVersion$)
20:     RouteTrafficAll($previousVersion$)
21:     ActivatePipelineVersion($previousVersion$)
22:     NotifyOperators("Rollback completed")
23: **end procedure**

This framework encodes systematic decision checkpoints leveraging automated monitoring and routing, ensuring controlled pipeline promotions. The rollback procedure guarantees the fallback to stable versions while minimizing downtime and preserving service continuity.

Managing complete ML pipeline versioning alongside multi-stage deployments equips engineering teams with the tools to orchestrate safe, traceable, and reproducible machine learning delivery. By harmonizing component versioning, dependency management, staged rollouts, and rollback strategies, organizations can confidently escalate models and pipelines from experimentation to production while preserving system resilience and auditability.

6.5. Automated Testing and Monitoring Hooks

In contemporary data processing and machine learning pipelines, proactive detection and remediation of defects are paramount to maintaining system integrity and performance. Embedding automated testing, validation, and monitoring hooks systematically throughout the pipeline enables early issue detection and supports continuous system improvement and operational robustness.

Automated tests integrated at various pipeline stages serve as the first line of defense against regressions and errors. These tests typically range from unit tests verifying individual components to integration tests assessing interactions across system modules. Unit tests validate deterministic functions such as data cleansing routines, feature engineering methods, and model inference code. Integration tests ensure that data flows correctly between stages, transformations preserve desired format and semantics, and model deployment interfaces behave as intended. Including schema validation tests at input boundaries, for instance, guarantees that incoming data conforms to expected types, ranges, and completeness before proceeding downstream.

Validation layers embedded directly after model training are critical to assess model quality and performance metrics with respect to predefined thresholds. Such validation includes checking statistical properties of predictions, ensuring absence of data leakage by verifying feature distributions, and performing fairness or bias assessments according to domain constraints. Automating these checks within continuous integration and delivery (CI/CD) workflows enforces quality gates that must be passed before model promotion, preventing degradation of live systems.

Monitoring hooks implanted in production pipelines provide continuous observation of model and system behavior under real operational conditions. They enable detection of performance degradation, data drift, and anomalous patterns in real time or near-real time. Performance monitoring involves tracking metrics such as latency, throughput, resource utilization, and prediction accuracy against historical baselines. Any deviation signaling system slowdown or quality issues triggers alerts for rapid investigation.

Drift detectors examine changes in data distribution or model input features over time relative to training data. Methods include statistical hypothesis tests (e.g., Kolmogorov–Smirnov test, population stability index) and distance-based measures (e.g., Wasserstein distance) applied to feature embeddings or raw input distributions. Detection of drift alerts teams to retrain or recalibrate models, thereby maintaining accuracy and relevance in dynamic environments.

Health indicators extend beyond model-centric metrics to encompass system-level signals such as error rates, environment conditions, and dependency availability. These indicators rely on application performance monitoring (APM) tools, log analysis, and custom probes integrated within pipeline components. For example, monitoring data source freshness and connectivity ensures data ingestion continues uninterrupted, reducing risk of stale or missing data downstream.

The design of these automated hooks prioritizes minimal performance impact and high observability. Instrumentation often uses
asynchronous logging and lightweight sampling to balance overhead with visibility. Furthermore, standardized interfaces and
telemetry formats facilitate aggregation and correlation across
pipeline stages, enabling holistic system diagnosis.

```python
from scipy.stats import ks_2samp
import numpy as np
import logging

class DriftDetector:
    def __init__(self, baseline_data):
        self.baseline = baseline_data

    def detect(self, new_data):
        # Apply Kolmogorov-Smirnov test feature-wise
        drift_flags = []
        for i in range(new_data.shape[1]):
            stat, p_value = ks_2samp(self.baseline[:, i],
    new_data[:, i])
            drift_flags.append(p_value < 0.05)
        return any(drift_flags)

def monitor_predictions(predictions, baseline_preds):
    detector = DriftDetector(baseline_preds)
    if detector.detect(predictions):
        logging.warning("Data drift detected in model inputs.")
    else:
        logging.info("No significant data drift detected.")

# Usage within the inference step
new_batch = np.random.rand(100,10)    # Incoming data batch
baseline_batch = np.random.rand(1000,10)  # Historical baseline
    data

monitor_predictions(new_batch, baseline_batch)
```

```
INFO:root:No significant data drift detected.
```

In addition to automated testing and monitoring within code, visualization dashboards play a vital role in presenting system health
and model behavior to engineers and stakeholders. Tools such as
Grafana, Kibana, or specialized ML observability platforms ren-
der performance trends, alert statuses, and data quality metrics on
real-time or historical bases. This comprehensive visibility enables

data teams to quickly respond to emerging issues and prioritize improvements.

Continuous integration systems are best leveraged to trigger testing and validation steps automatically upon code commits or data updates. For example, integration with tools like Jenkins or GitHub Actions enables pipeline stages to execute predefined test suites and report health metrics without manual intervention. Coupling automated alerts with incident management processes further ensures systematic issue tracking and resolution.

Embedding automated testing and monitoring hooks embodies the principles of DevOps and MLOps frameworks, emphasizing automation, repeatability, and rapid feedback. It replaces ad hoc manual checks with enforceable policies that safeguard reliability even as system complexity grows. This approach also aligns with regulatory and compliance requirements that mandate robust verification and traceability in data-driven applications.

Ultimately, a layered strategy combining rigorous tests, real-time monitoring, and thoughtful instrumentation cultivates resilience and agility in pipeline operations. Early detection of issues-whether introduced by code changes, data anomalies, or environment perturbations-minimizes downtime and mitigates risk. Over time, these automated checks generate valuable telemetry facilitating continuous performance improvement, adaptive model management, and trustworthy deployment at scale.

6.6. Hybrid Cloud and Multi-Environment Deployments

The complexity of modern machine learning (ML) workflows demands deployment strategies that transcend the confines of single infrastructures. Hybrid cloud and multi-environment deployments have emerged as essential paradigms, enabling organizations to leverage disparate resources-public clouds, private clouds, and on-premises environments-in a cohesive manner. This section examines architectural patterns and operational principles that facilitate the deployment, management, and scaling of ML pipelines across heterogeneous environments, balancing flexibility, cost efficiency, and global reach.

At the core of hybrid and multi-environment ML deployments lies the concept of decoupling compute, storage, and orchestration layers to enable portability and interoperability. A prevailing architectural approach involves containerization of ML components using technologies such as Docker, which encapsulate ML models, preprocessing steps, and inference services into immutable, environment-agnostic images. These container images are orchestrated via Kubernetes clusters that span multiple cloud providers and on-premises data centers, often facilitated by Kubernetes Federation or service meshes to achieve seamless discovery, load balancing, and failover.

Key to this architecture is the adoption of platform-agnostic workflow orchestration frameworks like Kubeflow Pipelines or Apache Airflow. These platforms provide declarative pipeline definitions, modular component reuse, and platform-independent execution capabilities. By abstracting the underlying infrastructure, ML practitioners can define end-to-end pipelines once and deploy them on multiple targets without substantial modification. Coupled with infrastructure-as-code tools such as Terraform or Pulumi, teams automate consistent environment provisioning, thus mitigating drift and accelerating repeatability.

Resource management is critical in hybrid scenarios to optimize utilization and contain costs. A common pattern involves tiered workload placement where latency-sensitive or compliance-bound workloads reside on-premises, while cost-intensive batch training leverages scalable public cloud GPU instances. Data locality considerations influence such decisions to reduce egress costs and data transfer latency. For instance, training on large datasets may occur within cloud object storage, whereas inference services for sensitive data remain on-premises behind strict access controls.

Networking strategies underpinning multi-environment deployments must address connectivity, security, and traffic routing across geographically distributed resources. Software-defined wide-area networking (SD-WAN) and dedicated private links (e.g., AWS Direct Connect, Azure ExpressRoute) establish secure, high-throughput connections that enable consistent data and metadata synchronization. Encrypted tunnels and strong identity federation ensure authentication and authorization policies are uniformly enforced across environments, supporting compliance requirements such as GDPR or HIPAA.

To maintain observability and operational control at scale, ML pipelines require distributed monitoring and logging solutions. Implementing metrics collection through Prometheus exporters, centralized log aggregation with Elasticsearch-Logstash-Kibana (ELK), or cloud-native monitoring services enables unified visibility over heterogeneous deployments. Alerting and anomaly detection mechanisms can be configured to trigger cross-environment remediation workflows, facilitating rapid fault isolation and recovery.

Scaling ML workflows in hybrid contexts demands elastic orchestration capable of dynamically reallocating resources based on workload demand and cost profiles. Autoscaling policies, informed by real-time telemetry, adapt compute resources across clusters. For example, Kubernetes Cluster Autoscaler can add nodes on cloud clusters during peak training jobs and scale down during idle periods, whereas on-premises resources may be statically provisioned or shared among multiple teams. Additionally, the use of spot/preemptible instances in clouds provides cost optimizations for interruptible workloads, with checkpointing integrated into the pipeline to handle disruptions gracefully.

Data synchronization mechanisms are fundamental to consistency and reliability across the hybrid ecosystem. Techniques such as distributed file systems (e.g., Lustre, Ceph) or cloud-native data replication services enable synchronization of input datasets, model artifacts, and feature stores. Event-driven architectures employing message queues (e.g., Kafka, RabbitMQ) facilitate asynchronous updates, triggering pipeline stages across environments upon data arrival. This supports continuous integration and continuous delivery (CI/CD) practices tailored for ML, reducing time-to-production while maintaining data integrity.

Security considerations permeate every aspect of hybrid and multi-environment deployments. Role-based access control (RBAC), fine-grained network policies, and data encryption both at rest and in transit are baseline requirements. Secrets management solutions, including HashiCorp Vault or cloud-managed key stores, ensure that credentials and sensitive configuration parameters are neither exposed nor hardcoded. Furthermore, audit logging and compliance automation tools ensure traceability of pipeline executions, model versions, and data transformations for governance.

Hybrid cloud and multi-environment deployment architectures also facilitate global scaling by enabling geo-distributed inference and training. By deploying inference endpoints closer to end-users in regional cloud zones or on-premises edge clusters, latency and bandwidth costs are minimized. Federated learning represents a cutting-edge pattern within this domain, allowing decentralized model training across multiple edge locations or data silos without consolidating data, thereby preserving privacy while improving model generalization.

Successfully deploying ML pipelines in hybrid cloud and multi-environment scenarios entails a combination of containerization, orchestrated workflow abstraction, strategic resource placement, robust networking, and continuous monitoring. These architectural choices empower organizations to achieve agility, cost-effectiveness, compliance adherence, and operational resilience, transforming distributed infrastructure into a unified ML platform capable of addressing complex, large-scale use cases.

Chapter 7

Security, Compliance, and Enterprise Readiness

Machine learning success at scale demands more than just accurate models—it requires unwavering security, rigorous compliance, and operational resilience. In this chapter, uncover how MLflow transforms from a versatile experiment tracker into a trusted enterprise backbone, insulating sensitive data, supporting legal mandates, and withstanding real-world threats. From identity and policy enforcement to audited, always-on deployments, this is your blueprint for responsible and robust ML operations.

7.1. Identity and Access Management

Integrating MLflow within an enterprise environment necessitates robust identity and access management (IAM) to ensure secure operation, compliance, and effective governance. This integration typically involves coupling MLflow with existing enterprise identity providers (IdPs) and single sign-on (SSO) solutions, thereby centralizing authentication and authorization processes. This section explicates the key principles and configuration practices to achieve such integration, focusing on secure authentication, role mapping, and enforcement of the principle of least privilege for both human users and automated systems interacting with MLflow.

MLflow does not natively handle authentication; rather, authentication is usually offloaded to external services via reverse proxies or middleware supporting standards such as OAuth2, OpenID Connect (OIDC), or SAML. Common enterprise IdPs such as Microsoft Azure Active Directory, Okta, or Google Workspace enable seamless identity federation and SSO capabilities, allowing users to authenticate once and gain access to multiple resources without repeated credential input.

To integrate MLflow with an IdP, the recommended architecture places a proxy layer such as NGINX or Apache HTTP Server configured with `mod_auth_oidc` or `mod_auth_mellon` fronting the MLflow tracking server and registry. This proxy intercepts all incoming requests, redirecting unauthenticated users to the IdP login page. Upon successful authentication, it verifies tokens or assertions and injects user identity details, typically via HTTP headers, to downstream MLflow services.

A representative example of an NGINX configuration snippet enabling OIDC authentication is:

```
location /mlflow/ {
    auth_request /oauth2/auth;
    error_page 401 = /oauth2/sign_in;

    proxy_pass http://localhost:5000/;
    proxy_set_header Host $host;
    proxy_set_header X-User $http_x_auth_request_user;
}
```

```
location = /oauth2/auth {
    proxy_pass http://oauth2_proxy/auth;
    proxy_set_header Host $host;
    proxy_pass_request_body off;
    proxy_set_header Content-Length "";
}
```

Here, the proxy forwards authentication requests to an OAuth2 proxy service integrated with an enterprise IdP. After authentication, authorized user attributes propagate as headers to MLflow.

Authentication alone does not establish user permissions; authorization necessitates precisely mapping authenticated identities or groups to role definitions within MLflow. Enterprise identity platforms typically maintain user group memberships, roles, or claims that reflect organizational permissions and responsibilities.

Effective role mapping requires:

- Extracting relevant identity claims from incoming tokens or assertions, such as group memberships or predefined role attributes.

- Translating these claims into MLflow roles, e.g., "Admin", "Editor", "Viewer", with granular permissions on experiment creation, model registration, deployment, or metadata modification.

This mapping is often implemented in the proxy layer or an API gateway that handles authorization. For example, the OAuth2 proxy can be configured with the --pass-authorization-header and claims-based mapping rules directing MLflow privileges.

Moreover, MLflow deployments can enforce role-based access control (RBAC) by verifying headers injected by the proxy and applying policy checks before executing sensitive functions. This approach decouples authentication and authorization concerns and leverages the enterprise IdP's group management features to simplify user management.

The principle of least privilege mandates that identities-both human operators and automated services-receive only the access rights necessary to perform their tasks, reducing the risk surface from inadvertent or malicious misuse.

Applying this principle in MLflow IAM entails:

- Defining minimal privilege roles aligned with job functions. For example, data scientists may be granted experiment and run creation rights but denied model deployment permissions, which are reserved for DevOps engineers.

- Implementing fine-grained permission scopes controlled by the access proxy or middleware, restricting actions such as reading metadata, modifying experiment parameters, or deleting runs.

- Distinguishing between user and machine identities, assigning scoped service accounts or application credentials with constrained capabilities for automation workflows, CI/CD pipelines, or monitoring agents.

When automated systems interact with MLflow-in unattended batch jobs or model retraining pipelines-mutual TLS, API tokens, or OAuth2 client credentials can be used for service authentication. These credentials are scoped narrowly to avoid exposure of sensitive operations. Rotation policies and audit logging further reinforce least privilege safeguards.

In practice, integrating MLflow IAM with enterprise IdPs involves a synthesis of configuration steps:

1. **Configure External Authentication Proxy.** Deploy and configure a reverse proxy incorporating OIDC or SAML modules that handle user authentication against the IdP.

2. **Token and Claim Extraction.** Ensure decoded tokens

pass user identity and group claims as HTTP headers to MLflow, e.g., X-User and X-Groups.

3. **Authorization Enforcement.** Customize MLflow or middleware to parse these headers and enforce RBAC policies, rejecting unauthorized operations.

4. **Configure Automation Credentials.** Create dedicated service accounts in the IdP with API client credentials scoped by role; inject these into automation environments.

5. **Audit and Monitoring.** Enable logging on proxy and MLflow to trace authenticated actions for compliance and anomaly detection.

Leveraging enterprise IAM capabilities for MLflow benefits security and operational efficiency; however, it also introduces considerations:

- *Token Expiry and Renewal*: Ensure tokens have suitable lifetimes balancing usability and security. Automate token refresh in client tools.

- *Header Forgery Prevention*: The proxy must strip or control sensitive headers to prevent spoofing downstream services.

- *Fail-Safe Defaults*: Deny access by default in case of authentication or authorization failures to minimize security risks.

- *Policy Consistency*: Align MLflow IAM policies with broader organizational policies to avoid discrepancies and ensure auditable access control.

Through careful integration of MLflow with enterprise IAM and SSO infrastructures, organizations can establish robust identity assurance, enforce stringent access controls, and maintain compliance-all essential for secure machine learning operations at scale.

7.2. Data Protection, Privacy, and Encryption

Data protection in modern enterprise environments mandates a comprehensive approach encompassing encryption, privacy enforcement, and safeguarding of both data content and its associated metadata. The increasing volume and sensitivity of information handled require rigorous controls that address data at rest, data in transit, and the often-overlooked metadata and artifacts that can inadvertently leak critical details.

Encryption of data at rest refers to securing information stored on persistent media, including file systems, databases, and cloud storage. Encrypting data at rest serves as a fundamental control against unauthorized access, particularly in scenarios where physical security controls might be circumvented or where storage is outsourced.

Practical implementations of encryption at rest typically involve full disk encryption (FDE), file-level encryption, or column-level encryption in database environments. Full disk encryption protects entire storage volumes, generally employing symmetric-key algorithms such as AES (Advanced Encryption Standard) with 256-bit keys to maximize security and performance balance. File-level encryption provides more granular protection, permitting selective encryption of sensitive files, while database encryption can isolate sensitive columns to minimize exposure risks.

Key management in encryption at rest is paramount. Keys must be stored separately from the data and managed securely through hardware security modules (HSMs) or dedicated key management services (KMS). Rotating keys periodically, applying role-based access controls (RBAC) to key usage, and maintaining audit trails form critical elements of an effective data at rest encryption strategy.

Encryption of data in transit covers any information moving across networks, including internal and external communications. Pro-

166

tecting this data involves preventing interception, tampering, and replay attacks, commonly achieved through transport layer security protocols.

TLS (Transport Layer Security) is the de facto standard for securing data in transit on the internet and enterprise communications. TLS operates by establishing a secure channel via a handshake process that authenticates parties and negotiates encryption parameters. Strong cipher suites using AES-GCM and forward secrecy mechanisms such as ephemeral Diffie-Hellman key exchanges ensure robustness against future cryptographic compromise.

Scenarios extending beyond typical web traffic may involve VPNs (Virtual Private Networks), IPsec tunnels, or application-layer encryption protocols (e.g., Message Layer Security-MLS). In all cases, adherence to up-to-date protocol versions and periodic security assessment of cipher suites is essential, as older standards (e.g., SSL, TLS 1.0) have known vulnerabilities.

Ensuring privacy mandates focus on limiting data exposure through minimization, pseudonymization, and anonymization techniques. By reducing the scope of personal or sensitive data collected, enterprises diminish risk vectors and ease compliance burdens.

Data minimization involves collecting only data strictly necessary for the identified purpose, while pseudonymization replaces direct identifiers with reversible tokens or hashes. Anonymization achieves irreversible transformation, rendering individuals unidentifiable, thus alleviating the applicability of regulations such as the GDPR.

Techniques such as differential privacy add noise to datasets, preserving aggregate utility while protecting individual identities in statistical analyses. Synthetic data generation further offers privacy-preserving alternatives to sharing real production data in testing or machine learning workflows.

Protection of metadata and artifacts is vital because metadata-data about data-often contains rich contextual information, including file names, timestamps, user access logs, and geolocation. Artifacts such as cryptographic signatures, audit logs, and configuration files also require protection, as exposure can lead to significant information leakage or manipulation.

Encrypting metadata alongside data is not always straightforward, particularly in systems requiring indexing or search capabilities. Strategies include format-preserving encryption or property-preserving encryption schemes that maintain functional operability without exposing plaintext metadata.

Audit logs, which track access and modification events, must be protected via cryptographic integrity checks such as hash chains or digital signatures to prevent tampering. Ensuring non-repudiation in security events is critical for incident investigation and regulatory compliance.

Compliance frameworks, such as the General Data Protection Regulation (GDPR), Health Insurance Portability and Accountability Act (HIPAA), and Payment Card Industry Data Security Standard (PCI DSS), impose stringent data protection obligations. Enterprises must integrate encryption and privacy controls into a holistic governance model encompassing policies, procedures, and technologies.

Mandatory requirements often include:

- Encryption of sensitive personal or financial data both at rest and in transit.

- Strict key management and access controls.

- Secure audit trails with evidence of encryption and access attempts.

- Data subject rights support, such as data portability and erasure.

- Periodic risk assessments and penetration testing focusing on encryption robustness and data leakage.

The deployment of automated compliance monitoring tools that verify encryption status and privacy controls can enhance accountability and reduce the risk of violations.

Implementing robust data protection necessitates a layered approach:

- **Classify Data:** Establish a data classification framework to identify and prioritize sensitive information that requires encryption.

- **Integrate Encryption Seamlessly:** Utilize native encryption capabilities provided by storage and communication platforms, augmented with custom encryption where necessary.

- **Centralize Key Management:** Use centralized, secure key management to facilitate policies, allow key rotation, and reduce operational errors.

- **Leverage Hardware Security:** Employ hardware-based security mechanisms, including trusted platform modules (TPMs) and HSMs, for enhanced cryptographic operations.

- **Monitor and Audit:** Continuously monitor encryption status and access events; maintain immutable logs for forensics and compliance.

```
from cryptography.hazmat.primitives.ciphers.aead import AESGCM
import os

key = AESGCM.generate_key(bit_length=256)
aesgcm = AESGCM(key)

nonce = os.urandom(12)
data = b"Sensitive enterprise data to encrypt"
aad = b"associated_data"
```

169

```
ciphertext = aesgcm.encrypt(nonce, data, aad)
```

```
# ciphertext contains the encrypted data, which includes integrity authentica
tion.
```

The convergence of encryption, privacy principles, and artifact protection forms a cornerstone of any effective enterprise data protection strategy. Rigorous application of these controls ensures confidentiality, integrity, and compliance in complex regulatory environments while safeguarding both data and the invaluable metadata that contextualizes it.

7.3. Audit Logging and Traceability

Comprehensive audit logging is a cornerstone of secure and reliable technology systems, providing an immutable and verifiable record of user actions, system events, and access to critical resources such as data models. The immutability and completeness of these logs underpin operational transparency, forensic investigations, and regulatory compliance. This section elaborates on the principles behind creating robust audit logs, the technologies and methodologies ensuring their integrity, and practical approaches to achieve exhaustive traceability.

Audit logs capture a sequence of events reflecting interactions between users, applications, and system components. Each entry typically includes a timestamp, actor identification, type of action performed, target resource, and outcome status. To guarantee the logs' utility, it is vital to ensure that they are tamper-resistant, comprehensive, and structured to support efficient retrieval and analysis. These characteristics enable organizations to reconstruct timelines of activity, identify anomaly patterns, and provide evidence during audits or incident response.

The immutability of audit logs can be enforced through several complementary techniques. Append-only storage systems restrict modifications to existing entries, allowing only new entries to be appended. This can be implemented using write-once-read-many (WORM) media or employing cryptographic mechanisms such as hash chaining. Hash chaining involves computing a cryptographic hash for each new log record combined with the hash of the previous record, forming a chain where any alteration to earlier entries disrupts the chain's integrity. This approach resembles blockchain principles applied internally for logs, offering strong guarantees against undetected tampering.

Consider a simplified example of hash chaining for log records:

```python
import hashlib
import json
import time

def hash_record(record, prev_hash):
    record_str = json.dumps(record, sort_keys=True) + prev_hash
    return hashlib.sha256(record_str.encode()).hexdigest()

log = []
prev_hash = "0" * 64  # Initial hash

def add_log_entry(action, user, resource):
    global prev_hash
    record = {
        'timestamp': time.time(),
        'action': action,
        'user': user,
        'resource': resource
    }
    record_hash = hash_record(record, prev_hash)
    log_entry = {
        'record': record,
        'hash': record_hash,
        'prev_hash': prev_hash
    }
    log.append(log_entry)
    prev_hash = record_hash

add_log_entry("access_read", "alice", "model_123")
add_log_entry("modify_write", "bob", "model_123")
```

The above method ensures that every log entry cryptographically depends on the prior entry, safeguarding the sequence from unauthorized modification.

Traceability extends beyond the mere collection of logs; it encompasses the ability to link user identities, performed actions, resource states, and system responses over time. Modern auditing frameworks incorporate contextual metadata such as session identifiers, IP addresses, device fingerprints, and authorization scopes, which collectively facilitate comprehensive forensic analysis. Integration with identity and access management (IAM) systems is critical to maintain accurate user attribution and mitigate risks related to impersonation or privilege escalation.

For environments involving machine learning or data models, audit logs must track access not only to raw data but also model training, evaluation, deployment, and inference activities. This is essential because models encapsulate learned behavior that can impact decision-making processes; thus, their lifecycle events constitute significant operational events. Capturing parameters such as model version, training dataset fingerprints, hyperparameters, and execution context enables reproducibility and accountability.

Tools supporting audit logging and traceability often provide capabilities for log aggregation, indexing, and querying. Solutions based on the ELK (Elasticsearch, Logstash, Kibana) stack or Splunk allow organizations to centralize logs from disparate systems, apply real-time search and anomaly detection, and visualize access patterns. These tools also facilitate alerting on suspicious or unauthorized activities, reinforcing proactive security postures.

To comply with diverse regulatory standards such as GDPR, HIPAA, or SOX, audit logs must meet specific criteria:

- Retention policies ensuring availability over mandated periods,

- Encryption both at rest and in transit to protect confidentiality,

- Access controls to prevent unauthorized log disclosure or manipulation,

- Periodic integrity checks and automated lifecycle management to sustain log relevancy and reliability.

In distributed or cloud-native architectures, achieving full traceability can be challenging due to system complexity and dynamic resource allocation. Incorporating distributed tracing methodologies alongside audit logging aids correlation of requests across microservices and infrastructure layers. Standards like OpenTelemetry specify instrumentation formats and protocols to collect telemetry data encompassing traces, metrics, and logs, enabling holistic visibility into system operations.

Implementing a comprehensive, immutable audit logging framework with enriched contextual metadata and strong cryptographic protections is imperative for full traceability. Leveraging appropriate tools and aligning practices with compliance requirements ensures operational transparency, facilitates investigations, and bolsters security governance within advanced technology environments.

7.4. Scaling for High Availability and Disaster Recovery

Ensuring maximum uptime in MLflow deployments necessitates a strategic combination of high availability (HA) and disaster recovery (DR) design principles. These principles must be meticulously integrated into both cloud and on-premises environments to guarantee uninterrupted service amid failures. High availability focuses on minimizing downtime by incorporating redundancy and automated failover mechanisms, while disaster recovery targets service restoration after catastrophic events. The following detailed examination addresses scalable architectures, clustering techniques, redundancy strategies, automated failover methods, and recovery procedures tailored to MLflow's operational requirements.

Clustering and Redundancy

At the core of a high-availability MLflow deployment lies clustering-the distribution of MLflow services across multiple interconnected nodes to prevent single points of failure. The MLflow tracking server, which manages experiment metadata and artifact locations, must be deployed in a cluster configuration supporting stateless frontends and durable backend storage.

To implement clustering, several components require redundancy:

- **MLflow Tracking Server Instances:** Deploy multiple instances behind a load balancer. This approach allows client requests to be redirected seamlessly if an instance fails. Each server instance should be stateless, delegating state persistence to the backend.

- **Backend Database:** The database (e.g., PostgreSQL, MySQL) holding experiment metadata must be highly available. Setting up a database cluster with synchronous replication ensures that transaction logs are propagated across multiple nodes, allowing rapid failover without data loss.

- **Artifact Storage:** Artifacts-large ML model binaries, datasets, and logs-are stored in object stores such as Amazon S3, Azure Blob Storage, or distributed file systems like HDFS. Object stores inherently provide redundancy and durability; hence, reliance on these services improves resilience.

The consistency of metadata and artifact storage underpins the HA architecture. For on-premises deployments, distributed databases such as Galera Cluster for MySQL or Patroni-managed PostgreSQL clusters provide synchronous replication and automatic failover capabilities critical for preserving metadata consistency. Similarly, leveraging Ceph, MinIO, or an NFS cluster for artifact storage ensures durability through replication.

Automated Failover

Automated failover mechanisms detect node or service outages and transparently reroute traffic or switch to standby resources without manual intervention. For MLflow deployments, automated failover must be applied both at the service and infrastructure layers.

On the service layer, the tracking server cluster should be fronted by a load balancer configured with health probes. When an instance becomes unresponsive, the load balancer removes it from the pool, distributing client requests only to healthy nodes. In cloud environments, managed load balancers (e.g., AWS Elastic Load Balancer, Google Cloud Load Balancing) offer native health checks and seamless failover. For on-premises, HAProxy, NGINX, or F5 Big-IP can fulfill this role with customizable probe intervals and circuit breaker patterns.

At the database layer, the failover process involves automatic leader election among cluster nodes. Tools such as Patroni utilize distributed consensus protocols (e.g., Raft) to maintain cluster state and orchestrate promotions of replicas to primary automatically. These tools integrate with orchestrators like Kubernetes or systemd to restart failed services promptly.

For artifact storage, failover is primarily handled by the storage service itself. When employing cloud object storage, its built-in replication ensures artifacts remain accessible despite node failures. In self-hosted storage, synchronization tools such as RADOS for Ceph or multiple MinIO nodes configured with erasure coding and replication safeguard against data loss and facilitate failover.

Disaster Recovery Procedures

Disaster recovery strategies complement high availability by addressing scenarios where service interruption exceeds the tolerance of failover mechanisms-such as datacenter-wide outages, major security incidents, or catastrophic hardware failures. Effective disaster recovery requires regular backups, geographic distribution, and tested recovery workflows.

Regular Backups

Backup policies must include both metadata and artifact data:

- **Metadata Backups:** Periodic snapshots of database state ensure that in the event of data corruption or failure, a consistent recovery point exists. Logical backups (e.g., `pg_dump` for PostgreSQL) combined with physical snapshots of database volumes allow flexible restoration options.

- **Artifact Backups:** Although object stores generally provide high durability, it is prudent to configure lifecycle policies to replicate artifacts across regions or to an alternative object store. For on-premises systems, periodic replication to offsite storage or tape backups protects against data center failures.

Geographic Distribution

Deploying active-active or active-passive replicas across geographically distinct locations diminishes the impact of region-specific disasters. In cloud environments, cross-region replication of both the database and artifact store is supported natively or through managed services. On-premises, WAN-accelerated replication tools facilitate near real-time synchronization between data centers.

Recovery Workflow

A documented, automated recovery workflow significantly reduces mean time to recovery (MTTR). This workflow includes:

- Validation of backup integrity.

- Restoration of the database to an agreed recovery point.

- Restoring artifact store access, either from cloud buckets or replicated storage.

- Redeployment or redirection of MLflow tracking endpoints.

- Verification of system health and client connectivity.

Infrastructure-as-code (IaC) tools and container orchestration platforms enhance recovery speed. Versioned deployment manifests capture the full state of MLflow services, enabling rapid recreation in alternate environments.

Cloud versus On-Premises Considerations

While core principles of HA and DR remain consistent, the implementation differs between clouds and on-premises settings.

Cloud Environments

Cloud providers offer managed services that simplify high availability:

- Managed relational databases with multi-AZ automatic failover.

- Global object storage with strong consistency and cross-region replication.

- Native load balancers and autoscaling groups.

- Managed Kubernetes clusters for orchestrating MLflow service pods with health checks and self-healing.

Cloud also facilitates rapid disaster recovery by provisioning infrastructure in new regions, significantly reducing recovery time.

On-Premises Environments

On-premises demands more intricate setup and maintenance:

- Deploying and managing database clusters using open-source tools requires operational expertise.

- Artifact storage must be architected using distributed storage solutions with replication.

- Load balancers require manual configuration and monitoring.

- Disaster recovery depends on local and remote backup infrastructure, often requiring custom automation scripts.

These environments benefit from hybrid models connecting on-premises systems to cloud backups or disaster recovery sites, combining best attributes of both.

Summary of Best Practices

Key guidelines for architecting MLflow deployments for HA and DR include:

- Deploy multiple stateless MLflow tracking server instances behind a load balancer.

- Use a highly available, clustered database with synchronous replication and automated failover.

- Leverage durable, replicated object storage for artifact persistence.

- Implement health monitoring and automated failover mechanisms at both the service and database levels.

- Establish comprehensive backup and disaster recovery work-flows, including geographically distributed replicas where possible.

- Utilize cloud-managed services when available for simplified scalability and recovery.

- In on-premises settings, employ mature open-source cluster-ing and replication tools with robust monitoring.

- Automate recovery processes using IaC and orchestration platforms to minimize downtime.

Strategic application of these methods ensures that MLflow de-ployments remain resilient, scalable, and capable of sustaining enterprise-level production workloads with minimal service inter-ruption.

7.5. Vulnerability Management and Hardening

Effective vulnerability management and system hardening con-stitute foundational pillars in securing an MLflow deployment against an evolving threat landscape. Given MLflow's role in man-aging machine learning lifecycles—tracking experiments, packag-ing code, and deploying models—ensuring proactive threat detec-tion, rigorous software patching, secure configurations, compre-hensive code scanning, and runtime hardening is imperative for maintaining data integrity and operational resilience.

Proactive Threat Detection

Early identification of threats requires continuous monitoring through automated tools and manual auditing. Integration with security information and event management (SIEM) systems enables collecting logs from MLflow server components, underlying infrastructure, and access controls. Establishing alerting rules to detect anomalous behavior—such as repeated failed login attempts, unexpected API call patterns, or unusual data access timing—facilitates rapid response. Leveraging machine learning-based anomaly detection can augment these efforts by identifying patterns outside established baselines, a capability well aligned with an MLflow-centric environment.

Software Patching and Dependency Management

One of the most frequent entry points for attackers exploits unpatched vulnerabilities in software or dependent libraries. MLflow, being a Python-based platform with numerous external dependencies, requires meticulous management of its software stack. Maintaining an up-to-date environment involves:

- Regularly consulting official MLflow releases and their security advisories.

- Employing tooling such as `dependabot` or `safety` to identify and remediate vulnerable Python packages.

- Implementing automated dependency scanning in continuous integration (CI) pipelines to detect both direct and transitive vulnerabilities before deployment.

Scheduled patch cycles must be balanced with operational availability; hence, engaging canary deployments or staging environments for testing patches minimizes risk before promoting updates into production.

Secure Configuration Best Practices

An insecure default or misconfigured environment substantially elevates risk. The following hardening practices directly improve MLflow's security posture:

- **Authentication and Authorization**: Enable strong authentication mechanisms, such as OAuth or LDAP integration, in front of MLflow APIs, enforcing least privilege by defining granular roles and permissions.

- **Transport Layer Security**: Configure MLflow's server endpoints behind reverse proxies employing TLS to encrypt data in transit, preventing man-in-the-middle and eavesdropping attacks.

- **Server Hardening**: Minimize the attack surface by disabling unused plugins and endpoints within MLflow and the hosting environment. Apply principles of network segmentation, restricting access to MLflow instances to trusted subnets or VPNs.

- **Storage Security**: Encrypt artifact stores—whether local filesystems, object storage (like S3), or databases—and employ access controls to prevent unauthorized artifact retrieval or tampering.

Documenting configurations as code supports repeatability and auditability, enabling rapid recovery from misconfigurations or breaches.

Code Scanning and Security Analysis

MLflow interacts heavily with codebases and models, necessitating thorough static application security testing (SAST) and dependency analysis. Integration of code scanning tools into the development lifecycle increases resilience against injection attacks, insecure deserialization, or leakage of sensitive data.

```
# Run Bandit to analyze MLflow project source code
bandit -r my_mlflow_project/ -f html -o bandit_report.html
```

```
Run started:2024-04-26 10:22:34

Test results:
[high] Use of exec detected on line 42
[medium] No asserts allowed outside tests on line 75
```

```
[low] Use of insecure MD5 hashing on line 128

Run metrics:
Total issues (by severity):
High: 1
Medium: 1
Low: 1

Code scanned:
Total lines: 1250
Files skipped: 0
```

Coupling such SAST outputs with dynamic application security testing (DAST) and dependency vulnerability scans forms a comprehensive assessment model. Moreover, scanning configuration files (e.g., YAML, JSON) used by MLflow for experiment tracking and deployment ensures credentials or secrets are not embedded inadvertently.

Runtime Hardening

Runtime hardening protects the MLflow environment from active exploitation and limits damage if a compromise occurs. Key tactics include:

- **Containerization and Isolation**: Deploy MLflow services in containers with minimal privileges, leveraging orchestrators like Kubernetes to enforce resource limits and network policies that isolate instances.

- **Mandatory Access Controls**: Use security frameworks such as AppArmor or SELinux to restrict MLflow processes' capabilities and system calls.

- **Runtime Integrity Monitoring**: Implement tools that detect binary or configuration file tampering in real time, alerting on changes that may indicate compromise.

- **Memory Protection Techniques**: Apply mitigations like Address Space Layout Randomization (ASLR), stack canaries, and control flow integrity on the host environment to reduce susceptibility to buffer overflows or code injection.

Runtime defense mechanisms should be continuously updated and tested against emerging exploits tailored to machine learning infrastructure, ensuring an adaptive security posture.

Preparing MLflow for the Evolving Cybersecurity Landscape

The security environment is dynamic, driven by increasing adversarial sophistication and expanding attack surfaces. Future-proofing an MLflow deployment involves establishing a feedback loop where:

- Threat intelligence—specific to machine learning environments and cloud-native platforms—is actively consumed and integrated into security controls.

- Regular penetration testing actively probes for weaknesses unavailable to automated scanners.

- Incident response plans incorporate scenarios involving data poisoning, model theft, and pipeline sabotage, all risks unique to ML workflows.

- Security awareness programs for data scientists and engineers emphasize best practices in coding, experiment tracking, and artifact management.

By embedding these strategies into standard operational procedures, MLflow instances can maintain robust defenses, swiftly adapt to threat evolution, and minimize potential damage from successful attacks. This multilayered approach to vulnerability management and hardening transforms MLflow from a functional platform into a secure, resilient cornerstone of machine learning infrastructure.

7.6. Enterprise Policy Enforcement and Governance

Establishing rigorous policy enforcement and governance within machine learning lifecycle management is imperative for ensuring compliance with organizational standards, legal regulations, and ethical principles. MLflow's extensible architecture and workflow automation capabilities provide robust mechanisms to embed policy controls directly into experimentation, model development, and deployment pipelines. This integration empowers organizations to maintain oversight, auditability, and consistency across complex ML activities while minimizing manual intervention and error-prone processes.

At the core of enterprise policy enforcement is automating the validation of organizational rules concerning model approval, data classification, and handling practices. Approval controls, for instance, can be implemented by extending MLflow's tracking and model registry components with programmatic gates. These gates verify that critical criteria are satisfied before model progression to subsequent stages such as staging or production deployment. Validation can include performance thresholds, adherence to defined fairness metrics, or the successful completion of security scans. An exemplary implementation could leverage MLflow model registry's transition request hooks, enforced via custom event listeners or orchestrated workflows in Kubernetes or CI/CD pipelines.

Labeling policies form an essential component within governance, enabling systematic classification of datasets, experiments, and models for compliance and operational clarity. By standardizing metadata tags such as `data_sensitivity`, `model_owner`, or `compliance_status` within MLflow tracking URIs, data scientists and engineers can maintain visibility over how assets conform to organizational mandates. Automating these labels relies on integrating external policy decision points that evaluate attributes such as data provenance, geographic restrictions, or consent. For example:

```
import mlflow

def enforce_labeling_policy(run_id):
    with mlflow.start_run(run_id=run_id) as run:
        dataset_sensitivity = check_data_sensitivity(run.data.
    params["dataset_uri"])
        mlflow.set_tag("data_sensitivity", dataset_sensitivity)
        compliance_status = determine_compliance(run.data.params)
        mlflow.set_tag("compliance_status", compliance_status)

def check_data_sensitivity(dataset_uri):
    # Interface with data catalog or classification service
    if "PII" in query_data_classification_service(dataset_uri):
        return "high"
    return "low"

def determine_compliance(params):
    if params.get("region") in ["EU", "UK"]:
        return "GDPR-compliant"
    return "non-compliant"
```

This programmatic enforcement guarantees that every experiment run is annotated consistently, simplifying downstream audits, access control, and automated policy enforcement.

Handling sensitive data requires aligned technical and legal safeguards embedded within ML workflows. Enforcing data governance principles in MLflow mandates integrating data access policies directly into experiment initialization and artifact management. Access to sensitive datasets can be restricted by incorporating pre-run validation hooks that examine user credentials and data classification tags before permission is granted. Combined with data encryption and fine-grained artifact access controlled by service-level authorization, MLflow provides a framework to operationalize data handling mandates such as HIPAA, GDPR, or internal confidentiality protocols.

A comprehensive governance framework also involves validating conformity to ethical mandates, such as fairness and bias mitigation. Automated fairness checks can be executed as part of the model validation step, embedding these validations into MLflow workflows to prevent models with unacceptable bias profiles from advancing. A typical fairness-checking function is integrated after model training and before deployment, with results stored as model registry metadata to document compliance evidence:

```
def evaluate_fairness(model, test_dataset):
    metrics = compute_fairness_metrics(model, test_dataset)
    if metrics["demographic_parity_difference"] > 0.1:
        raise Exception("Fairness threshold exceeded")
    mlflow.set_tag("fairness_metrics", metrics)

def compute_fairness_metrics(model, dataset):
    # Implement fairness metrics calculations (e.g., parity
    difference)
    return {"demographic_parity_difference": 0.05}
```

Enforcing these checks within MLflow's automated workflows bridges technical operations with organizational ethical policies, ensuring that models deployed in production adhere to defined standards beyond mere performance metrics.

Integration with enterprise-wide governance platforms or policy engines further enhances automation. Policy-as-code tools such as Open Policy Agent (OPA) can be orchestrated alongside MLflow to evaluate complex policies expressed in high-level declarative rules. These evaluations can be triggered through REST API calls or CLI commands encapsulated within CI/CD pipelines managing MLflow workflows, ensuring that each model lifecycle stage complies with evolving regulatory landscapes and internal protocols.

Additionally, all policy enforcement actions and decisions should be logged immutably in audit trails maintained within MLflow's tracking server and augmented by external systems if necessary. Transparent record-keeping is indispensable for regulatory audits, forensic investigations, and continuous compliance improvement cycles.

In sum, embedding enterprise policy enforcement within MLflow workflows requires:

- Programmatic gating mechanisms for model transitions and approval controls.

- Automated and consistent metadata labeling tied to data governance and compliance requirements.

- Integration of data handling validations ensuring adherence to legal and security protocols.

- Embedded ethical mandate validations, including bias and fairness checks.

- Orchestration with external policy-as-code frameworks for scalable governance.

- Comprehensive audit trail recording to facilitate transparency and accountability.

This multifaceted approach ensures that ML operations not only deliver technical excellence but rigorously respect organizational mandates, empowering enterprises to scale ML innovation with confidence and control.

Chapter 8

Observability, Monitoring, and Cost Optimization

Building great ML models is just the beginning—ensuring they perform reliably, efficiently, and cost-effectively in production is where real value is realized. In this chapter, explore how MLflow unlocks deep visibility and control over operational health and spend, letting you anticipate issues, automate responses, and maximize business impact. Master the tools and techniques to watch your pipelines—and your budget—with confidence.

8.1. Instrumentation and Metrics for MLflow Services

Effective instrumentation and monitoring are critical components in managing MLflow services at scale. Capturing rich operational metrics allows engineering teams to maintain service reliability, optimize performance, and gain insights into user interactions and system behavior. These metrics range from low-level system resource utilization to high-level API request patterns, each providing a distinct perspective on the health and efficiency of MLflow deployments.

At the core of instrumentation is the integration of metric collection mechanisms within the MLflow service architecture. MLflow, typically deployed with components such as tracking servers, model registry, and REST APIs, should expose internal state and external interaction data continuously. The first step involves embedding instrumentation hooks to capture key events and resource statistics.

System-level metrics are foundational for understanding the operational environment. Monitoring CPU consumption, memory usage, disk I/O, network throughput, and file descriptor counts empowers operators to detect bottlenecks or resource exhaustion early. Common approaches include exposing these metrics through the Linux /proc filesystem or leveraging libraries like psutil in Python environments where MLflow components run.

An exemplary metric gathering snippet in Python for CPU and memory might resemble:

```
import psutil

def get_system_metrics():
    cpu_percent = psutil.cpu_percent(interval=1)
    mem = psutil.virtual_memory()
    mem_percent = mem.percent
    return {'cpu_percent': cpu_percent, 'memory_percent':
     mem_percent}
```

Such data should be emitted at configurable intervals (e.g., every 10 seconds) and pushed to a central time-series database or monitoring system.

MLflow services expose RESTful APIs enabling functionalities like experiment tracking, run logging, and model registration. Instrumenting these endpoints involves capturing request metadata including timestamps, response statuses, latencies, and payload sizes. This instrumentation facilitates latency profiling, error rate tracking, and usage pattern analysis, which are essential for capacity planning and SLA management.

Middleware or decorator patterns are commonly employed to wrap API handlers and collect these metrics seamlessly. For instance, using Python's Flask framework:

```
from time import time
from flask import request
from prometheus_client import Summary, Counter

REQUEST_LATENCY = Summary('mlflow_request_latency_seconds', '
    Request latency')
REQUEST_COUNT = Counter('mlflow_request_count', 'API request
    count',
                        ['method', 'endpoint', 'http_status'])

@app.before_request
def start_timer():
    request.start_time = time()

@app.after_request
def record_metrics(response):
    latency = time() - request.start_time
    REQUEST_LATENCY.observe(latency)
    REQUEST_COUNT.labels(request.method, request.path, response.
    status_code).inc()
    return response
```

Here, prometheus_client serves as a client library for exporting metrics to Prometheus, a widely-adopted monitoring system.

To maintain scalability and reliability, it is vital to adopt systematic practices for metrics collection:

- **Standardized Metric Naming and Labels:** Employ consistent and descriptive naming conventions. Include labels (dimensions) capturing details such as environment (prod, staging), region, or service component to enable granular filtering.

191

- **Sampling and Aggregation:** High-frequency events, such as individual API calls during peak load, may overwhelm storage and processing pipelines. Utilize sampling strategies or aggregate at the source to reduce dimensionality.

- **Metric Types Appropriateness:** Use counters for cumulative events (e.g., total requests), gauges for current values (e.g., memory usage), histograms or summaries for distributions (e.g., request latency).

- **Health Checks and Alerts:** Define health check metrics and thresholds for critical parameters. Propagate these to alerting systems to enable proactive incident response.

Visualization tools transform raw metric data into actionable insights. Dashboards built with systems like Grafana provide real-time views and historical trends. Effective dashboards for MLflow services should incorporate:

- **Resource Utilization Panels:** CPU, memory, disk, and network metrics for all key infrastructure layers.

- **Request Metrics Overview:** Total request volume, error rates (4xx, 5xx codes), and latency percentiles (p50, p90, p99).

- **Experiment and Model Performance Correlations:** Overlaying operational metrics with ML experiment throughput, run durations, and registry activities can reveal system load impacts.

Integration with log aggregation platforms, such as the ELK stack (Elasticsearch, Logstash, Kibana), further enriches monitoring by correlating logs with metrics, enabling comprehensive root cause analysis.

For advanced diagnostics, distributed tracing can be incorporated to track request flow through multiple MLflow microservices or supporting infrastructure. OpenTelemetry provides a vendor-neutral framework for capturing traces and spans, which, when correlated with metrics, reveal latency sources and bottlenecks in complex distributed setups.

Instrumentation should propagate trace context identifiers across API calls, database queries, and internal RPCs.

A robust MLflow monitoring architecture thus consists of:

- Embedded instrumentation libraries within MLflow services to emit metrics.

- Exporters forwarding these metrics to centralized systems such as Prometheus.

- Aggregation pipelines reducing noise and enabling efficient storage.

- Visualization and alerting platforms (e.g., Grafana) for operational insights.

- Optional tracing frameworks for granular request flow examination.

Consistent application of these principles facilitates proactive management of MLflow environments, enabling teams to sustain high availability, optimize resource consumption, and enhance user experience through robust observability.

8.2. Monitoring Model Performance in Production

Monitoring the performance of machine learning models in production environments is paramount to ensure the sustained reliability, accuracy, and efficiency of deployed systems. Once a model is operational, tracking its behavior under real-world conditions becomes essential not only to uphold service level agreements (SLAs) but also to promptly detect and mitigate potential issues that could degrade its utility.

Three core performance dimensions require continuous observation in deployed models: latency, throughput, and prediction quality.

Latency measures the time taken from receiving a request to producing a prediction. Low latency is critical for real-time and user-interactive applications. Excessive latency may lead to poor user experience or downstream system timeouts.

Throughput quantifies the number of requests a model serves per unit time, reflecting scalability and capacity. Bottlenecks that restrict throughput can cause queuing delays or request drops under load.

Prediction Quality assesses the accuracy and relevance of model outputs against expected or ground truth values. Quality degradation can arise from data drift, model decay, or unforeseen input distributions, necessitating retraining or model revision.

These metrics provide a comprehensive view of both operational and inferential aspects of model health, ensuring that the system meets technical and business objectives.

Effective monitoring demands rigorous instrumentation of the inference pipeline. Implementing lightweight yet informative tracing enables collection of timestamps, request identifiers, input data summaries, and output statistics. This information supports downstream aggregation and analysis without imposing significant overhead.

Typical instrumentation methods include:

- *Middleware Wrapping*: Intercept inference requests and responses at service entry and exit points for latency and throughput timing.

- *Custom Logging*: Emit structured logs capturing metadata about inputs, predictions, confidence scores, and error codes.

- *Metrics Exporters*: Integrate with metrics systems (e.g., Prometheus, StatsD) to export counters and gauges reflecting request counts and durations.

The choice of instrumentation technology must balance data granularity, transmission latency, and system resource consumption.

Real-time dashboards consolidate metric streams into visual interfaces that enable continuous oversight. They empower operators and data scientists to perceive trends, anomalies, and emergent issues through intuitive graphs, tables, and alerts.

A robust dashboard design for model monitoring typically includes:

- **Latency Percentiles**: Display median, 95th, and 99th percentile latencies to capture distribution characteristics and outlier behavior.

- **Request Rates**: Show throughput as requests per second with temporal granularity to identify traffic patterns or sudden load spikes.

- **Prediction Accuracy Metrics**: For classification, track measures such as F1-score, precision, and recall computed over rolling time windows using real-time labels when available.

- **Error and Failure Rates**: Visualize the occurrences of failed predictions, timeouts, or exceptions.

- **Resource Utilization**: Include CPU, memory, and GPU usage statistics to correlate performance bottlenecks with system constraints.

Open-source platforms such as Grafana, along with cloud-native monitoring solutions, facilitate customizable and scalable dashboard deployment.

Detecting failures and degradations proactively is critical to maintaining SLA compliance and minimizing downtime.

Threshold-Based Alerts: Set static or adaptive thresholds on key metrics (e.g., latency exceeding 200 ms, error rate above 1%) to trigger notifications. While straightforward, thresholding requires careful tuning to balance sensitivity and false positives.

Anomaly Detection: Employ statistical or machine learning methods to identify deviations from expected model behavior without predefined thresholds. Techniques include moving average comparisons, control charts, or unsupervised learning for multivariate anomalies.

Drift Detection: Monitor shifts in input data distributions or feature importance using metrics like population stability index (PSI) or Kullback–Leibler divergence. Detecting concept or data drift early enables timely retraining or model switching before prediction quality diminishes significantly.

Synthetic Load and Canary Testing: Deploy shadow or canary releases of updated models running concurrently with production to compare performance under controlled conditions, highlighting regressions before full rollout.

To ensure compliance with SLAs that mandate availability and response time guarantees, monitoring systems must integrate with incident management workflows. Automated escalation and remediation mechanisms facilitate rapid recovery from detected failures.

Strategies include:

- *Redundancy and Auto-Scaling*: Elastic infrastructure can adjust capacity dynamically based on throughput metrics to prevent bottlenecks.

- *Circuit Breakers and Failover*: Temporarily disable faulty model endpoints and route requests to fallback models or cached predictions.

- *Continuous Retraining Pipelines*: Trigger model updates upon detected data drift or quality degradation to maintain accuracy over time.

Consider a real-time image classification system deployed on a cloud platform. Instrumentation employs middleware to record start and end timestamps for each request and emits structured JSON logs via Fluentd to an Elasticsearch cluster. Prometheus scrapes metrics exported by the inference service, including counters for total requests, failed predictions, and latency histograms.

A Grafana dashboard displays:

- Latency percentiles over the last 15 minutes with color-coded heatmaps.

- Request rate line graph depicting peak and off-peak usage.

- A rolling 1-hour confusion matrix analyzing predicted labels versus ground truth from human-in-the-loop verifications.

- Alert panels indicating when latency routinely exceeds SLA limits or error rates spike unexpectedly.

Alerts trigger automated emails and webhook calls to incident response bots, escalating to on-call engineers if the abnormal state persists beyond a configured grace period.

Persistent and comprehensive monitoring of machine learning models in production is a multifaceted endeavor involving meticulous data collection, intelligent visualization, and proactive alerting mechanisms. By focusing on latency, throughput, and prediction quality through real-time dashboards, complemented with early failure detection techniques, organizations can ensure continual operational excellence and adherence to SLAs. This approach nurtures model trustworthiness and enables adaptive management in dynamic production landscapes.

8.3. Drift Detection and Alerting

In dynamic production environments, static models degrade as the statistical properties of input data or relationships they leverage evolve over time. Traditional up/down monitoring alone fails to capture these subtleties. Detecting and addressing both data drift and model drift is essential for sustaining the accuracy and reliability of predictive systems. This section delineates effective patterns for implementing drift detection mechanisms and robust alerting frameworks, which are crucial for adaptive model management.

Drift manifests in two primary forms: *data drift* and *model drift*. Data drift, sometimes called covariate shift, occurs when the feature distribution in production differs significantly from the training data distribution. Model drift refers to a degradation in the model's predictive performance, typically caused by changes in the underlying relationship between features and target variables, such as concept drift or label shift.

Quantitatively, consider a feature vector $\mathbf{X} \in \mathbb{R}^d$ and a label Y. Data drift is indicated by changes in the marginal distribution $P_{\text{prod}}(\mathbf{X})$ relative to $P_{\text{train}}(\mathbf{X})$, whereas model drift often arises from a change in conditional distribution $P_{\text{prod}}(Y|\mathbf{X}) \neq P_{\text{train}}(Y|\mathbf{X})$.

Data drift detection relies on statistical hypothesis testing and distribution comparison techniques. Several tools and metrics are employed for this purpose:

- **Population Stability Index (PSI):** Measures shifts in feature distributions by comparing binned frequency distributions. PSI values above a threshold (commonly 0.2) indicate significant drift.

- **Kolmogorov–Smirnov (KS) Test:** A non-parametric test that quantifies the maximum distance between empirical cumulative distribution functions (CDFs) of feature samples from training and production.

- **Jensen–Shannon Divergence (JSD):** A symmetric and bounded measure of similarity between probability distributions, useful when detecting smooth changes.

- **Multivariate Drift Detection:** Techniques like multivariate KS tests or Maximum Mean Discrepancy (MMD) extend detection to joint distribution changes across multiple features simultaneously.

Practically, the implementation involves segmenting production data into windows (e.g., daily or batch-based) and continuously comparing these distributions against baseline training distributions.

Model drift is harder to detect directly without access to ground truth labels. A common approach involves proxy metrics and validation strategies:

- **Performance Monitoring:** Tracking model accuracy, precision, recall, or AUC on recent labeled data. Declines beyond statistically significant bounds imply model drift.

- **Unsupervised Proxy Metrics:** When labels are delayed or unavailable, monitoring prediction confidence distributions, entropy, or changes in predicted class proportions can signal anomalies.

- **Shadow / Champion-Challenger Models:** Deploy a parallel model trained continuously on recent data to compare outputs. Divergence in predictions indicates potential drift.

- **Feature Attribution Stability:** Analyzing shifts in feature importance or SHAP (SHapley Additive exPlanations) values over time to detect changing model behavior.

Effective drift detection is embedded within scalable data pipelines and operational workflows. Key patterns include:

- **Batch Monitoring Pipeline:** Periodically aggregate production data, compute relevant statistics and drift metrics, and maintain historical logs for trend analysis.

- **Online / Streaming Detection:** Utilize incremental algorithms and sliding windows to identify drift promptly in streaming data environments, enabling near real-time responses.

- **Hybrid Approaches:** Combine both batch and streaming methods, exploiting the stability of batch analysis with the agility of online monitoring.

- **Metadata Enrichment:** Annotate data with timestamps, environment tags, and model versions to correlate drift events with system changes or external factors.

Drift detection must be paired with a responsive alerting system to enable timely interventions:

- **Threshold-Based Alerts:** Define domain-specific thresholds on drift metrics or performance degradation. Exceeding these thresholds triggers automated notifications.

- **Multi-Level Alerting:** Design alerts with escalating severity-warnings for marginal drift and critical alerts for significant or persistent changes.

- **Integration with Incident Management:** Connect alerts to ITSM (IT Service Management) platforms or incident response tools for coordinated action.

- **Automated Remediation Actions:** Implement conditional workflows where alerts can trigger model retraining, feature recalibration, or rollback to a previously validated model.

For instance, an alert rule based on PSI scoring could be specified as:

```
psi_threshold = 0.2

def check_psi(feature_psi):
    if feature_psi > psi_threshold:
        alert_message = f"Data drift detected: PSI={feature_psi
        :.3f}"
        send_alert(alert_message)
        trigger_model_evaluation()
```

```
Output example:
Alert triggered: Data drift detected: PSI=0.275
Initiating model performance evaluation workflow.
```

Implementing drift detection and alerting faces several challenges:

- **Label Availability:** Timely access to true labels is often limited, necessitating unsupervised or proxy drift signals.

- **False Positives and Sensitivity:** Balancing sensitivity and specificity is critical to avoid alert fatigue and maintain operational trust.

- **Feature Correlation and High Dimensionality:** Multivariate correlations complicate drift detection; dimensionality reduction or embedding techniques may help.

- **Concept Evolution vs. Noise:** Discriminating between meaningful concept drift and transient noise requires sophisticated statistical modeling and domain insights.

Adhering to the following best practices improves system robustness:

- Regularly update baseline distributions and performance baselines to reflect evolving environments.

- Implement layered monitoring across data input, intermediate features, and final predictions.

- Automate end-to-end drift detection with built-in provenance tracking for auditability.

- Continuously incorporate domain knowledge and regular validation cycles to refine drift thresholds and alerting criteria.

Collectively, these strategies enable proactive detection of hidden distributional shifts and emergent model deficiencies, preserving model efficacy while mitigating risks inherent to changing operational landscapes.

8.4. Resource Utilization and Cost Profiling

The effective management of machine learning (ML) pipelines necessitates a thorough understanding of the consumption patterns of compute, storage, and input/output (I/O) resources. Profiling these aspects not only facilitates cost optimization but also informs capacity planning and scaling strategies, ensuring robust and efficient deployment at scale.

Compute utilization in ML pipelines is primarily driven by model training and inference workloads, which often demand substantial

CPU or GPU cycles. High granularity profiling tools capture metrics such as CPU utilization percentage, GPU core usage, memory bandwidth, and execution times of individual operations or kernels.

Profiling starts by instrumenting the pipeline to log resource consumption per task or stage. For instance, during training, it is essential to observe parameters like per-epoch execution time and GPU memory allocation. Aggregating these metrics across runs enables the identification of bottlenecks, such as underutilized hardware or inefficient parallelization strategies.

Consider the following example using a profiling API:

```
import torch
from torch.profiler import profile, record_function,
    ProfilerActivity

with profile(activities=[ProfilerActivity.CPU, ProfilerActivity.
    CUDA],
              record_shapes=True, with_stack=True) as prof:
    with record_function("model_inference"):
        model(input_tensor)

print(prof.key_averages().table(sort_by="cuda_time_total"))
```

This snippet captures CPU and GPU activity during model inference, providing a tabular breakdown of time spent on individual operations. By isolating costly functions, practitioners can optimize or refactor code segments accordingly.

Storage profiling encompasses both persistent and ephemeral data storage. Persistent storage holds datasets, model checkpoints, and logs, while ephemeral storage often refers to caching mechanisms or temporary scratch space in distributed environments.

Quantitative analysis of storage includes measuring data read-/write throughput, latency, and volume across different storage tiers (e.g., SSDs, HDDs, object stores). Profiling tools that monitor file I/O operations can reveal excessive or redundant data transfers-for example, repeated loading of entire datasets instead of incremental updates or sampling.

A critical cost driver lies in checkpointing frequency and storage format. Frequent checkpoints increase storage overhead and I/O load, while inefficient serialization can inflate file sizes. Balancing checkpoint intervals with recovery requirements is essential to minimize both storage costs and downtime.

I/O profiling extends beyond local disk access to encompass the network layer, especially significant in distributed ML setups. Inter-node communication costs, data shuffling during distributed training, and remote data source access constitute primary I/O considerations.

Metrics such as bandwidth utilization, packet loss, and latency interrelate with overall pipeline throughput. Tools like Linux `perf`, `iostat`, or specialized telemetry agents can provide fine-grained statistics related to network and disk subsystems.

Identifying I/O bottlenecks requires correlating these statistics with workload patterns. For example, a sudden spike in network traffic during gradient aggregation implies potential inefficiencies in synchronization. Improving communication protocols (e.g., switching from TCP to RDMA) or employing gradient compression algorithms can substantially reduce network cost impacts.

Profiling resource utilization independently is insufficient without synthesizing these insights into cost profiles. Costs arise from the product of resource consumption and pricing schemes defined by cloud providers or on-premise accounting metrics.

An effective approach involves mapping resource consumption metrics onto dollar figures, enabling direct comparison between pipeline components. A cost breakdown report might list GPU hours, storage gigabytes, and network traffic, each monetized per current rates.

Analyzing such reports allows prioritization of optimization efforts.

Resource	Consumption	Unit Cost	Total Cost
GPU Compute	50 GPU-hours	$2.50 / GPU-hour	$125.00
Storage	200 GB-months	$0.10 / GB-month	$20.00
Network Egress	100 GB	$0.12 / GB	$12.00

Table 8.1: *Example cost profile for ML pipeline resources*

If GPU compute dominates costs, optimizing training algorithms or hardware utilization becomes critical. Conversely, if network charges are disproportionate, reducing data movement through caching or data locality strategies can be more effective.

Resource utilization patterns are foundational inputs to capacity planning. Accurate profiling ensures that scaling decisions-whether vertical (e.g., more powerful instances) or horizontal (e.g., adding nodes)-are justified by empirical data rather than heuristics.

Benchmarking resource metrics under varying workloads helps model scaling curves and predict saturation points. For example, tracking memory usage growth during training allows anticipating when model size or batch size adjustments necessitate upgraded hardware.

Dynamic scaling strategies, such as autoscaling clusters or spot-instance utilization, rely on real-time and historical profiling data to trigger expansion or contraction. Integrating resource monitoring with orchestration platforms enables workload-aware elasticity, ultimately reducing both costs and performance degradation risks.

Best practices for resource utilization and cost profiling involve:

- **End-to-End Instrumentation:** Employ comprehensive logging and monitoring at each pipeline stage.

- **Granularity and Aggregation:** Balance fine-grained metrics with higher-level aggregates to detect both localized inefficiencies and systemic trends.

- **Automation:** Integrate profiling and cost analytics into CI/CD workflows for continuous feedback.

- **Visualization:** Use dashboards to facilitate exploratory analysis of resource consumption patterns over time.

Popular tools supporting these practices include:

- `TensorBoard` and `Weights & Biases` for training and experiment profiling.

- Cloud provider native monitoring such as Amazon Cloud-Watch, Azure Monitor, and Google Cloud Monitoring.

- Open-source systems like Prometheus and Grafana for customizable metrics collection and visualization.

By embedding systematic resource utilization and cost profiling into ML pipeline development and operation, organizations can significantly reduce waste, improve performance, and better align infrastructure investment with application demands.

8.5. Usage Analytics for ML Experimentation

Effective management of machine learning (ML) experimentation relies heavily on comprehensive usage analytics that reveal critical dimensions of experimental activity. These analytics enable teams to uncover who is running experiments, the nature and distribution of these experiments, the emergence of bottlenecks in workflows, and pertinent interactions with underlying infrastructure. By leveraging such insights, organizations enhance process efficiency and promote optimal collaboration among users, thereby accelerating innovation cycles.

At its core, usage analytics in ML experimentation involves the systematic collection and aggregation of metadata generated by experiment tracking systems, resource schedulers, and version control platforms. Typical data points include user identities, timestamps, model configurations, dataset versions, compute environment parameters, experiment duration, and resource utilization. Extracting temporal and relational trends from this metadata requires sophisticated query mechanisms and visualization techniques tailored to the specificities of iterative ML workflows.

User Activity and Experiment Distribution Understanding the distribution of experiments across individuals and teams reveals participation levels and domain focus areas. Analytics dashboards commonly present metrics such as the number of experiments launched per user over selected intervals, experiment success rates, and frequency of parameter sweeps. For example, a sustained increase in experiments initiated by a particular subgroup might indicate emerging research interests or shifts in project priorities. Similarly, identifying underutilized personnel or resources highlights opportunities for improved training or resource reallocation.

Aggregation by geographic location or organizational unit can expose patterns of adoption and collaboration inefficiencies. If experiments are disproportionately concentrated in a single environment or region, this can point towards isolated silos that may benefit from improved cross-team communication. Visualization tools like heatmaps or Sankey diagrams aid in making such patterns intuitively graspable, facilitating management decisions aimed at balanced workload distribution.

Identification of Bottlenecks Bottlenecks in ML experimentation arise when constraints in compute power, storage, data availability, or workflow dependencies hinder progress. Usage analytics can pinpoint these choke points by analyzing temporal patterns such as queue lengths for experiment scheduling, average wait times for resource allocation, and failure rates correlated with specific infrastructure components. For instance, repeated experiment failures linked to a particular GPU cluster node or software environment version indicate the necessity for system maintenance or configuration updates.

Moreover, tracking the elapsed time between successive experimental phases (data preprocessing, model training, evaluation) can expose stage-specific delays that undermine pipeline efficiency. Statistical profiling of these intervals across multiple experiments helps prioritize optimization efforts. Automated alerts can be configured to notify system administrators or team leads when usage anomalies surpass defined thresholds, thus enabling proactive troubleshooting.

Infrastructure Usage and Resource Impact Granular monitoring of infrastructure interactions reveals how experiments consume compute, storage, and network resources. Key metrics include GPU/CPU utilization percentages, memory footprints, disk I/O patterns, and network throughput associated with individual experiments or user groups. Analysis of these metrics over time identifies resource contention and underutilization scenarios.

For example, experiments exhibiting excessive memory consumption without corresponding gains in performance efficacy may indicate suboptimal model architectures or data handling approaches. Additionally, spreadsheets or aggregated reports summarizing resource usage per project assist in cost accounting and budgeting for cloud or on-premises environments. Integrating these insights with infrastructure-as-code tools facilitates dynamic scaling policies and resource scheduling based on demand forecasts derived from historical usage.

Process Improvement Through Data-Driven Insights Combining user activity, bottleneck analysis, and infrastructure utilization data generates actionable intelligence that informs refinement of ML experimentation processes. One common application involves streamlining experiment orchestration workflows by introducing automated dependency resolution, adaptive resource provisioning, and prioritization mechanisms

208

for high-value experiments.

Empirical evidence of frequent experiment repetition due to lack of parameter tuning standardization can prompt the adoption of shared experiment configuration templates or centralized parameter repositories. Similarly, analytics highlighting redundant data transfers or inefficient data caching strategies motivate improvements in data pipeline architecture.

Collaboration enhancement emerges naturally from the visibility gained into experiment interdependencies and user interactions. Shared dashboards enable users to identify ongoing projects aligned with their expertise, fostering cooperative experimentation and knowledge exchange. Access controls and audit trails derived from usage analytics also contribute to maintaining data security and compliance without impairing collaborative openness.

Case Study: Optimizing Experiment Throughput in a Distributed Team Consider an enterprise ML team dispersed across multiple sites, utilizing a hybrid cloud infrastructure. By analyzing experiment submission logs, it was discovered that 70% of experiments were initiated by just two sub-teams, causing prolonged queue times for GPU resources. Detailed timeline analyses revealed that experiment setup phases, particularly data access and environment provisioning, accounted for over 40% of total experiment duration.

In response, the team implemented a centralized experiment queue with priority scheduling and deployed containerized environments with pre-installed dependencies. They also established a shared data caching layer to reduce redundant data transfers. Post-implementation analytics demonstrated a 35% reduction in average experiment turnaround time and increased experiment throughput without additional infrastructure investment.

Technological Enablers and Analytical Tools Advanced analytics for ML experimentation leverage a combination of telemetry collection frameworks, time-series databases, and interactive visualization platforms. Commonly used tools include Prometheus and Grafana for infrastructure monitoring, experiment tracking systems such as MLflow or Weights & Biases for capturing experiment metadata, and custom ETL pipelines for integrating disparate data sources.

Machine learning techniques themselves facilitate anomaly detection and predictive analytics on experiment usage metrics, enabling anticipatory resource management. Graph-based analysis uncovers complex experiment lineage and dependency mappings essential for reproducibility assessments and impact analysis of experimental changes.

Collecting, analyzing, and acting upon usage analytics in ML experimentation empowers organizations to identify and mitigate inefficiencies, balance experimental workloads, and optimize infrastructure utilization. This continuous feedback loop fosters an environment conducive to sustained innovation and collaborative advancement, ensuring experimentation resources are fully leveraged to meet evolving research and production demands.

8.6. Optimizing Storage and Artifact Lifecycle

Effective management of artifacts in software development and continuous integration environments demands a strategic approach to retention, archiving, and garbage collection. The artifact lifecycle, if left unmanaged, can lead to uncontrolled storage growth, inflated costs, and compliance risks. Optimizing this lifecycle requires balancing three critical constraints: regulatory compliance, cost efficiency, and high availability for ongoing and future use.

Retention policies form the foundation of artifact lifecycle management. These policies specify the duration and conditions under which artifacts are preserved, deleted, or archived. Retention intervals are often dictated by regulatory mandates such as GDPR, HIPAA, or industry-specific rules requiring traceability, auditability, and reproducibility. For example, financial software artifacts might need to be retained for several years, while rapid prototyping environments can enforce shorter retention spans. Implementing retention policies via automated workflows ensures consistency and reduces human error. Typical retention parameters include creation date, last access date, artifact version, and relevance to active projects.

Archiving complements retention by relocating stale but legally or operationally important artifacts to cost-effective, durable storage tiers. Archiving solutions leverage storage technologies optimized for infrequent access, such as cold cloud storage or object storage with lifecycle management policies. This transition reduces the occupancy of high-performance storage and lowers cost without compromising long-term accessibility. Archiving must support rehydration capabilities, enabling quick retrieval of artifacts for audits, debugging, or legal discovery. Metadata preservation and indexation during archiving are essential to maintain searchability and traceability across storage layers.

Garbage collection addresses the problem of artifacts that no longer serve any purpose. This task involves identifying artifacts eligible for deletion under retention guidelines and removing them permanently to free storage resources. Efficient garbage collection requires precise tracking of artifact dependencies and usage. For instance, artifacts associated with abandoned branches or deprecated versions can be flagged for cleanup. Reference counting and provenance analysis facilitate safe deletion, avoiding disruption caused by inadvertent removal of artifacts required by other builds or environments.

The orchestration of retention, archiving, and garbage collection is optimally managed through policy-driven automation integrated within the artifact repository system or continuous delivery pipeline. Defining and enforcing these policies declaratively allows seamless application across heterogeneous artifact types, build environments, and organizational units. Artifact lifecycle automation engines interpret these policies to schedule and execute storage actions, maintaining a sustainable balance between availability and cost.

Cost management hinges on understanding the storage cost components—capacity, access frequency, API request costs, and data transfer fees—in the chosen storage infrastructure. Cloud providers typically offer multiple storage classes with varying cost-performance trade-offs. When configuring retention and archiving policies, it is crucial to classify artifacts by their access patterns and business value. Hot artifacts actively used in development or deployment pipelines should remain on low-latency, high-throughput storage. Conversely, aged or low-priority artifacts can be transitioned to archival storage with lower costs but higher access latency.

The integration of analytics and monitoring tools enhances the visibility of artifact storage utilization and lifecycle efficiency. Key performance indicators such as storage growth rate, cost per artifact, access frequency, and policy compliance rates provide actionable insights. Periodic audits verify alignment with regulatory requirements and identify artifacts that warrant reclassification or deletion. Intelligent anomaly detection can highlight unexpected surges in artifact creation or retention violations, prompting immediate remediation.

Illustrative lifecycle management can be expressed as an algorithmic policy model, enforceable via repository automation. Consider the following pseudocode outlining a policy for artifact aging, archiving, and deletion:

```
For each artifact in repository:
    age = current_date - artifact.creation_date
```

```
if artifact.is_marked_for_permanent_retention():
    continue  # Skip deletion or archiving
else if age > deletion_threshold:
    if artifact.is_referenced():
        archive_artifact(artifact)
    else:
        delete_artifact(artifact)
else if age > archiving_threshold:
    archive_artifact(artifact)
```

In this model, thresholds are configurable parameters reflecting organizational policies. The function `is_referenced()` examines whether the artifact is still required by active builds or deployments. Archiving migrates eligible artifacts to a cost-effective tier while maintaining metadata integrity, and deletion reclaims storage without risking data loss for compliance needs.

Successful artifact lifecycle optimization ultimately reduces operational overhead, mitigates risk, and aligns storage expenditures with tangible business value. A mature approach involves continuous refinement of policies through feedback loops based on usage metrics, evolving compliance standards, and advances in storage technology. By harmonizing retention, archiving, and garbage collection within integrated automation frameworks, organizations can sustainably manage storage growth while preserving the long-term accessibility and integrity of critical build artifacts.

Chapter 9

Case Studies and Real-world Implementations

Explore the dynamic frontier where theory meets practice—this chapter is a guided tour through the diverse realities of deploying and scaling MLflow in the wild. From global enterprises to lean startups and edge devices, discover actionable lessons, design patterns, and cautionary tales shaped by success and adversity in production environments worldwide.

9.1. Enterprise-Grade MLflow Deployments

Large-scale adoption of MLflow within enterprise environments necessitates a convergence of sophisticated architectural design, rigorous governance, and cross-functional collaboration. Enterprise-grade deployments transcend the typical single-team use case, expanding to accommodate hundreds-if not thousands-of production models, diverse data science teams, and stringent compliance requirements. Analyzing real-world implementations reveals critical technical and organizational strategies that underpin the successful scaling of MLflow in complex organizations.

A notable example is a multinational financial institution managing over 300 machine learning models across varied domains such as credit risk, fraud detection, and customer segmentation. The bank adopted MLflow as its central tracking and lifecycle management platform to unify disparate experimentation workflows and ensure reproducibility. The technical infrastructure implemented a layered approach: a dedicated MLflow tracking server cluster backed by a distributed, highly available relational database optimized for metadata persistence and querying. This setup was complemented by scalable artifact storage utilizing object storage services with lifecycle policies aligned to compliance requirements.

Integration at scale relied heavily on the decoupling of experimentation from deployment pipelines. Data scientists interacted primarily with MLflow's Python and REST APIs to log experiments and models during their iterative workflows. Simultaneously, a separate MLOps engineering team developed modular, pipeline-driven deployment mechanisms that consumed MLflow model registries. This separation of concerns facilitated agility for data teams without compromising production stability and governance.

Governance was a critical challenge addressed through a combination of automated policy enforcement and human-in-the-loop processes. The organization extended MLflow's model registry capabilities by implementing custom validation hooks within the registration pipeline. These hooks performed automated compliance checks, verifying model lineage metadata, performance thresholds, and fairness criteria before permitting transitions from staging to production stages. Additionally, audit logs capturing all registry interactions were federated into the enterprise governance information system, providing traceability and regulatory reporting capabilities.

Managing hundreds of models required an advanced naming and versioning scheme to reflect cross-domain ownership and classification. The teams established explicit conventions incorporating model domains, business units, and lifecycle states directly into MLflow model names and tags. This facilitated intuitive querying and grouping via the MLflow UI and APIs, streamlining governance reviews and impact analyses. Furthermore, an internal cataloging service was developed to synchronize model metadata from MLflow with business glossaries and data dictionaries, reinforcing alignment between data science outputs and business language.

Another essential aspect was the orchestration of deployment and monitoring processes. The organization implemented event-driven pipelines triggered by model registry transitions using a message queue architecture. When a model was promoted to production in MLflow, corresponding deployment workflows were launched automatically, including container image creation, deployment to Kubernetes clusters, and integration with runtime monitoring tools. Continuous monitoring fed back into MLflow's tracking server by logging production metrics and service health indicators, enabling an end-to-end view of model lifecycle performance.

From an organizational perspective, the governance framework was underpinned by an enterprise-wide Center of Excellence (CoE) for machine learning. The CoE maintained the MLflow platform, defined best practices, and facilitated knowledge sharing. It also coordinated cross-functional committees comprising data scientists, compliance officers, and business stakeholders. These committees periodically reviewed model performance, risk assessments, and regulatory requirements, embedding business alignment into the operational fabric of ML workflows.

Real-world data science teams emphasized the importance of embedding reproducibility at scale. Automated pipelines handled environment management via containerization and infrastructure-as-code, enabling seamless recreation of experimental contexts. Artifacts such as feature engineering code, environment specifications, and training datasets were versioned and linked to experiment runs within MLflow, preventing drift and supporting auditability. This strategy was crucial not only for debugging and iterative improvement but also for satisfying regulatory expectations around model validation.

Another large-scale deployment context is an international e-commerce enterprise operating multiple ML teams across geographies and business units. Their MLflow infrastructure incorporated a multi-tenant architecture with role-based access controls (RBAC) at granular levels-ranging from project workspaces to model registry operations. This effectively segmented data science activities while maintaining centralized visibility. Integration with the enterprise identity and access management system ensured secure and auditable authentication.

To optimize resource utilization and reduce operational overhead, this organization embraced a federated model registry synchronization mechanism. Teams maintained local MLflow registries aligned with their workflows, while a centralized registry aggregated production-certified models. Synchronization agents periodically reconciled model metadata, preserving lineage, tags, and version histories. This hybrid approach balanced autonomy with governance, improving model reuse and reducing duplication.

In these enterprise deployments, adherence to strict SLAs and low-latency inference requirements prompted extensive integration of MLflow with CI/CD pipelines and scalable serving platforms. Models registered in MLflow triggered automated quality gates based on test suites and canary evaluations. When requirements were met, deployment pipelines updated serving endpoints with minimal downtime, embedding rollback capabilities and blue/green deployment strategies to mitigate operational risk.

Key learnings from these deployments highlight that MLflow's extensible architecture and rich API ecosystem are enabling factors for enterprise adoption rather than limitations. Successful scaling depends on tailoring MLflow's components to the organizational context through custom development, robust infrastructure design, and embedding governance at multiple layers-from metadata validation to business-aligned review processes. The adoption journey is inherently multidisciplinary, requiring synchronization of data science innovation, engineering rigor, compliance mandates, and strategic business objectives.

Enterprise-grade MLflow deployments represent a sophisticated blend of technology, process, and organizational adaptation. They demonstrate how a unified ML lifecycle platform can serve as the foundational bedrock for operational excellence and accountability at scale, transforming model management from isolated experiments to governed, production-grade assets aligned with enterprise strategy.

9.2. Scaling MLflow in Research and Academia

MLflow has rapidly become an essential tool in academic and research environments, where the imperatives of reproducibility, transparency, and collaboration are paramount. As research projects scale up in complexity and scope-spanning large-scale benchmarks, collaborative experiments, and extensive datasets-MLflow's platform capabilities provide critical infrastructure to address these challenges systematically.

A key requirement in academic research is the ability to conduct and share reproducible experiments. Reproducibility hinges on comprehensive tracking of code versions, data sources, experimental parameters, and environment configurations. MLflow's experiment tracking component systematically logs this metadata, enabling researchers to recreate any prior experiment with precise fidelity. By automating the capture of parameters, metrics, artifacts, and source control references, MLflow eliminates manual documentation errors and ensures that all aspects influencing experimental results are preserved. This rigorous provenance tracking supports peer review processes, allowing reviewers to validate findings or extend experiments on a consistent foundation.

Research consortia and academic labs increasingly focus on large-scale benchmarking studies to evaluate and compare machine learning methods across diverse datasets and problem domains. MLflow's model registry and automated pipeline integration facilitate such benchmarking by managing multiple model versions, coordinating evaluation workflows, and aggregating performance metrics. Within shared MLflow environments, standardized experiment templates and reproducible deployment configurations enable researchers to run benchmarks under controlled conditions, vastly reducing variability. The model registry further aids in cataloging state-of-the-art models and establishing baselines that serve the community. This infrastructure also accelerates meta-analyses and the synthesis of results vital for scientific publications.

Open science movements emphasize transparency and knowledge dissemination. MLflow promotes openness by enabling seamless sharing of models, results, and execution environments among collaborators and with the broader community. Research groups can export MLflow experiment artifacts, including logged models and environment Conda specifications, enabling others to reproduce results or build upon published work without excessive setup overhead. Platforms such as institutional repositories or public model hubs integrate with MLflow's artifact storage to ensure long-term accessibility and citation. This interoperability underpins the rigorous documentation requirements of open research and supports data and model availability statements increasingly mandated by journals and funding agencies.

Collaborative publishing workflows are also enhanced by MLflow's centralized tracking and registry. Multi-institutional teams working on joint publications can aggregate their experiments within shared MLflow workspaces, allowing contributors to monitor progress, compare experimental variants, and resolve discrepancies before paper submission. The ability to link specific MLflow runs to manuscript figures, tables, and code repositories encourages comprehensive documentation within manuscripts. Journals that adopt reproducible research standards benefit from authors providing MLflow experiment identifiers, which facilitate direct access to underlying experimental details for verification or further exploration.

From an operational perspective, academic institutions face unique challenges in scaling MLflow, including multi-user access control, resource management, and data governance. Deployments often integrate MLflow tracking servers with cluster computing environments or cloud platforms used for research. Role-based authentication and access policies ensure sensitive data and proprietary models remain protected while enabling wide collaboration. Moreover, tight integration with high-performance computing schedulers and data storage systems streamlines the execution of resource-intensive experiments and large data transfers essential for modern research workflows.

Successful adoption of MLflow in research also fosters a cultural shift toward a more disciplined and transparent scientific process. Researchers become more conscious of reproducibility principles, experiment documentation, and collaborative review. The standardized interfaces and automation provided by MLflow reduce repetitive administrative work and enable scientists to focus on hypothesis-driven inquiry and innovation. Over time, such tools contribute to building institutional knowledge bases, enriched with well-curated experiment histories that serve as references for new projects or educational purposes.

MLflow addresses fundamental scalability and reproducibility challenges in academic and research settings by providing a unified framework for experiment tracking, model management, and environment reproducibility. Its adoption supports rigorous benchmarking, open science standards, and collaborative publishing, while enabling institutions to manage resources and security effectively. Through these capabilities, MLflow strengthens the integrity and impact of machine learning research, advancing a culture of transparency, peer review, and knowledge sharing indispensable to scientific progress.

9.3. MLflow at the Edge and IoT

The deployment of machine learning (ML) models within edge and Internet of Things (IoT) environments introduces substantial complexity beyond conventional centralized cloud platforms. Unlike data centers with virtually unlimited computational resources and reliable network connectivity, edge devices and IoT nodes frequently operate under severe constraints in processing power, memory, storage, and communication bandwidth. This contextual shift mandates a rigorous reconsideration and adaptation of ML lifecycle management frameworks such as MLflow, originally designed for more resource-rich and continuously connected environments.

- Key challenges in adopting MLflow at the edge and in IoT deployments include intermittent or absent network connectivity, limited computational capacity for training or inference, and heterogeneous device capabilities that complicate uniform model deployment and monitoring. Furthermore, ensuring secure, consistent model versioning and governance across distributed fleets of edge nodes demands robust synchronization methods that minimize the volume and frequency of data exchanges.

- Offline training emerges as a critical paradigm when connectivity constraints prohibit real-time data streaming or remote model updates. In these situations, devices accumulate data locally for batch training cycles or inference model fine-tuning asynchronously. The constraints of scale and reliability also accentuate the importance of incremental and federated training approaches where devices contribute model updates without sharing raw data, maintaining privacy and reducing network burdens.

- **Lightweight Local Tracking and Logging**

  Directly porting MLflow's standard tracking server to edge devices is infeasible due to hardware limitations. Instead, lightweight local agents have been developed, capable of caching run metadata, metrics, parameters, and artifacts in compact, serializable formats. These local stores can buffer experiment metadata and model artifacts during offline periods, deferring synchronization until connectivity is restored.

  Data compression and schema-efficient serialization protocols (e.g., Protocol Buffers, Apache Arrow) are leveraged to reduce storage load and facilitate rapid transfer when network availability returns. Moreover, local MLflow clients can employ selective logging strategies that prioritize critical parameters and performance metrics, reducing resource consumption without sacrificing traceability.

- **Model Packaging and Deployment at Scale**

  MLflow Models' modular format is optimized for portability across heterogeneous runtimes, which is essential for IoT deployments. Edge-adapted MLflow workflows automate packaging models into minimal runtime containers or platform-specific binaries (e.g., TensorFlow Lite or ONNX runtime formats) to ensure compatibility with constrained devices.

223

Deployment pipelines integrate with device management services that track fleet topology, device health, and software versions. Models are deployed incrementally using canary releases or phased rollouts to subsets of devices to monitor performance and identify regressions, reducing risks in remote update scenarios.

- **Federated and Incremental Training Support**

  Exploiting MLflow in federated learning schemes involves coordinating local training on edge nodes and central aggregation of model updates. MLflow experiments record metadata on local training runs, hyperparameters, and model weights diffs rather than entire datasets, conserving bandwidth and safeguarding privacy.

  Scripts embedded in MLflow projects adapt to partial synchronization, enabling incremental integration of improvements from multiple nodes without immediate server interaction. This approach offers resilience to node dropout and network partitions, further accommodating edge dynamics.

- Efficient synchronization techniques form the backbone of MLflow's edge adaptations. In bandwidth-limited scenarios, delta or patch-based transfers of model parameters and metadata are favored over full replication. Metadata synchronization schedules take into account network cost, device power states, and urgency of updates, often implemented via event-driven or asynchronous architectures.

- Edge caching proxies and localized MLflow tracking servers may be deployed on intermediate network nodes to consolidate data from nearby devices before forwarding to central servers, thus amortizing connection costs. This multi-level hierarchy mirrors federated topologies and improves fault tolerance across unreliable communication channels.

- Edge and IoT environments present amplified security risks, including attack surfaces from physical access and exposure of device credentials. MLflow's integration with secured transport mechanisms (e.g., TLS) and access token management is extended to these distributed devices with additional layers such as hardware-backed key stores and secure enclaves.

- Data and model artifacts encoded with cryptographic signatures verify integrity during transit and deployment. Moreover, privacy-preserving mechanisms inherent in federated approaches alleviate concerns over transmitting sensitive data, aligning MLflow's experimental tracking with strict regulatory compliance in IoT data domains.

- Emerging implementations demonstrate MLflow's versatility in edge-driven real-world applications. For instance, industrial IoT scenarios utilize MLflow-adapted pipelines for predictive maintenance models running on factory floor sensors, where network isolation and latency preclude continuous cloud interaction. Similarly, smart agriculture systems deploy local training orchestrated by MLflow projects on autonomous weather stations, synchronizing model improvements when connectivity permits.

- These case studies underscore the necessity for robust offline mode capabilities, modular packaging formats, and asynchronous synchronization protocols within MLflow's architecture to meet the stringent demands posed by edge and IoT environments.

The convergence of these adaptations ensures that MLflow remains a practical and powerful tool for lifecycle management of machine learning models in distributed and resource-constrained edge contexts. By embracing minimalist local tracking, federated training protocols, and bandwidth-aware synchronization,

MLflow achieves a scalable orchestration of distributed IoT intelligence without compromising the essential transparency and reproducibility of ML experiments.

9.4. Startup Innovation with MLflow

Startups face unique challenges that emphasize the need for rapid innovation cycles, resource efficiency, and the seamless integration of machine learning (ML) workflows into business operations. In such fast-moving environments, MLflow emerges as a formidable toolset that accelerates the journey from model ideation to production deployment, empowering startups to maintain competitive agility while managing limited technical and financial resources.

MLflow's modular architecture encapsulates three core components: Tracking, Projects, and Models, that collectively streamline experimentation, reproducibility, and deployment. For startups prioritizing rapid prototyping, MLflow Tracking provides an accessible and centralized platform to log experiments, hyperparameters, and metrics. This capability enables data scientists to iterate swiftly, contrasting multiple model versions under varying conditions without losing traceability. The lightweight REST API and UI interface allow for easy integration with existing development pipelines, which is crucial for small teams aiming to maximize output without extensive overhead.

Lean experimentation, a hallmark of startup product development, benefits significantly from MLflow's experiment management. By automatically capturing environment details, dependencies, and execution contexts, startups ensure that each prototype is reproducible both locally and in cloud environments. Such reproducibility not only expedites debugging but also facilitates knowledge transfer across distributed or shifting teams, mitigating risks associated with personnel changes or scaling efforts. The ability to version control data and models simultaneously with code reduces technical debt by preserving the lineage from raw data through pre-processing to prediction, fostering transparency and enabling data-driven decision-making at every stage.

Continuous delivery of ML models, a critical factor for product responsiveness in startups, leverages MLflow Projects and Models. Projects provide a structured format for packaging code in a reusable and shareable manner, abstracting complexities of environment setup through specification files like `conda.yaml` or `Dockerfile`. This standardization enables quick transitions between experimental notebooks and production-grade codebases, bridging the gap between prototyping and deployment pipelines. Startups can automate testing and validation workflows using MLflow Projects combined with continuous integration (CI) systems, significantly reducing cycle times from code commits to live updates.

MLflow Models enhance deployment flexibility by supporting multiple serialization formats such as `python_function`, `ONNX`, and `TensorFlow`. In startup contexts, where infrastructure heterogeneity is common, this abstraction enables seamless integration with serving platforms, cloud managed services (e.g., AWS SageMaker, Azure ML), or edge devices without modifying core model logic. The deployment APIs simplify model serving and rollback, critical to maintaining user trust during frequent release cycles. Additionally, MLflow's built-in support for REST APIs and batch inference aligns well with serverless and microservice architectures often favored by startups for scalability and cost-efficiency.

Cost-effectiveness remains paramount in resource-constrained startup environments. MLflow's ability to unify disparate tools into a single, extensible platform reduces the operational burden and eliminates reliance on multiple costly, proprietary frameworks. Its open-source nature ensures accessibility without licensing fees while fostering a community-driven innovation ecosystem. Startups benefit from integrations with popular ML libraries (e.g., scikit-learn, PyTorch, XGBoost) and cloud storage backends, enabling affordable scaling of experiment tracking and model registry without dedicated infrastructure investments.

Automation and orchestration of ML workflows significantly enhance startup productivity. MLflow integrates smoothly with orchestration tools such as Kubernetes, Apache Airflow, and Prefect, enabling complex pipelines that incorporate data ingestion, training, evaluation, and deployment. This integration supports the continuous training paradigm, whereby models are regularly retrained with fresh data to adapt to evolving business needs or changing user behaviors. Such agility is indispensable for startups seeking product-market fit through incremental improvements rather than infrequent, large-scale releases.

Consider a hypothetical early-stage startup developing an AI-driven recommendation engine. Using MLflow, the data science team rapidly prototypes candidate algorithms with diverse feature sets and hyperparameters, each run systematically logged and compared through the MLflow UI. Once a promising model is identified, it is packaged via MLflow Projects and deployed as a REST endpoint using MLflow Models, enabling immediate feedback from live customer interactions. Automated retraining jobs triggered by new user data utilize the consistent experiment metadata from the MLflow Model Registry, ensuring smooth rollouts and quick rollbacks when required. This tightly integrated workflow empowers the startup to innovate continuously without sacrificing reproducibility or stability.

MLflow catalyzes startup innovation by combining agility, automation, and cost-effective model management into a cohesive platform optimized for the nuances of early-stage technology ventures. Its design philosophy addresses the critical need for rapid prototyping, iterative experimentation, and seamless continuous delivery, all within an ecosystem that scales gracefully as the startup matures. By reducing the complexity of ML lifecycle management and fostering reproducible, traceable workflows, MLflow enables startups to confidently leverage machine learning as a strategic differentiator in dynamic and competitive markets.

9.5. Complex Distributed Training Use Cases

Distributed training workflows in machine learning often transcend the confines of a single cluster, extending into multi-cluster and multi-data-center configurations. These scenarios introduce significant complexities in experiment management, artifact tracking, and lineage preservation. MLflow's architecture, with its modular and scalable design, facilitates coordination among distributed teams, enabling seamless handling of vast datasets and intricate workflows.

A prototypical complex use case involves an organization conducting hyperparameter optimization experiments across geographically dispersed clusters. Each cluster, equipped with specialized GPU nodes, concurrently explores distinct segments of the parameter space. MLflow's tracking server operates as a federated system, either deployed in a centralized cloud environment or as replicated instances synchronized via a backend database that supports multi-region replication, such as Amazon Aurora Global Database or Google Spanner.

By employing MLflow's REST API and MLflow Tracking SDK, distributed teams log experiments locally while syncing metadata with the central tracking server. This setup ensures consistent visibility and aggregation of experiment metrics and parameters across clusters. The artifact storage, decoupled from the tracking server, leverages cloud object stores (e.g., Amazon S3, Google Cloud Storage) accessible globally. This design choice accommodates large datasets and model binaries, enabling automatic versioning and secure access control.

Consider a multi-step training pipeline spanning clusters in different data centers, executing sequential stages such as data preprocessing, model training, and evaluation. Each stage generates datasets and artifacts critical for downstream stages and auditing. MLflow Projects encapsulate each stage within reproducible containers or conda environments, promoting modularity and reproducibility despite heterogeneous cluster environments. Integration with workflow orchestration tools (e.g., Kubernetes, Airflow) further automates pipeline execution while emitting MLflow run metadata at each stage.

The preservation of lineage across these distributed workflows is central to the traceability and auditability of model development. MLflow's experiment and run identifiers serve as stable anchors for correlating artifacts, parameters, and metrics across stages and clusters. Metadata tags provide semantic organization, supporting filtering by team, project, or deployment environment. This structured metadata schema facilitates root cause analysis and model governance, particularly in regulated industries.

An exemplary experiment scenario involves a team training models on petabyte-scale datasets partitioned across data centers to comply with data residency policies. Data subsets are ingested through distributed data lakes, and each subset undergoes localized feature extraction. MLflow's artifact logging captures feature store snapshots and intermediate model checkpoints, which are then aggregated asynchronously at a central repository. The system supports lineage queries enabling the reconstruction of complex dependencies, such as which data partition and feature configuration contributed to a particular trained model.

Advanced use cases often employ MLflow Model Registry to manage staged deployment across international production clusters. Models approved in one region trigger automated rollout procedures in adjacent regions, where testing and monitoring are performed using region-specific datasets reflective of local conditions.

This federated model lifecycle management is complemented by
MLflow's integration with continuous integration/continuous deployment (CI/CD) pipelines, maintaining synchronized registry
states despite asynchronous model promotion.

To illustrate, the following snippet presents a simplified code example simulating distributed experiment tracking across two clusters using MLflow's Python API. Each cluster logs runs independently to the same remote tracking server and uploads artifacts to
a shared S3 bucket.

```python
import mlflow
import mlflow.sklearn
from sklearn.ensemble import RandomForestClassifier
from sklearn.datasets import load_iris
from sklearn.model_selection import train_test_split

# Configure tracking URI pointing to centralized MLflow tracking
    server
mlflow.set_tracking_uri("https://mlflow-central.example.com")
experiment_name = "Distributed_Hyperparam_Search"
mlflow.set_experiment(experiment_name)

def train_and_log(random_state):
    # Load sample data
    data = load_iris()
    X_train, X_test, y_train, y_test = train_test_split(
        data.data, data.target, test_size=0.2, random_state=
    random_state)
    # Train model
    model = RandomForestClassifier(random_state=random_state,
    n_estimators=10)
    model.fit(X_train, y_train)

    # Log experiment run
    with mlflow.start_run():
        mlflow.log_param("random_state", random_state)
        mlflow.log_param("n_estimators", 10)
        acc = model.score(X_test, y_test)
        mlflow.log_metric("accuracy", acc)
        mlflow.sklearn.log_model(model, "model")

# Simulate parallel runs from two clusters with different random
    seeds
train_and_log(random_state=42)    # Cluster A
train_and_log(random_state=99)    # Cluster B
```

The centralized tracking URI coordinates the experiment metadata across multiple clients, while the shared artifact store guarantees that model binaries and logs remain accessible to all collaborators. This approach simplifies the aggregation of results and supports downstream analysis workflows.

MLflow's architectural components-centralized tracking server, distributed artifact stores, and model registry-enable robust management of complex distributed training scenarios. It empowers cross-functional teams to efficiently capture, share, and govern experimental metadata and artifacts, ensuring consistent lineage and reproducibility across diverse and large-scale machine learning workflows spanning clusters and data centers.

9.6. Lessons Learned: Pitfalls and Best Practices

In practical deployments of MLflow, a recurrent theme is the delicate balance between flexibility and reproducibility. Teams often face challenges related to version control, environment management, and experiment tracking consistency that can undermine the benefits MLflow promises if not addressed properly. A critical pitfall is inadequate governance of MLflow experiments: without enforced standards for naming, tagging, and artifact organization, projects quickly devolve into unmanageable complexity. This obscures lineage and impedes collaboration, especially in larger teams where multiple members simultaneously contribute and iterate.

A foundational best practice involves strict adherence to a unified experiment lifecycle policy. This consists of defining conventions for experiment and run naming schemes that reflect project, algorithm version, and key hyperparameters. For instance, embedding semantic versioning in experiment names facilitates rapid identification of meaningful differences across runs. Additionally, consistent use of tags to capture metadata such as data source versions, hardware specifications, or model intents ensures that runs remain self-descriptive and searchable within MLflow's tracking server. Automating these conventions at run submission time, via wrapper functions or pipeline orchestration tools, significantly reduces human error and enforces compliance.

Another frequent obstacle revolves around environment reproducibility. MLflow's built-in conda and Docker integration facilitate environment capture but require discipline. Without regularly updated environment specifications closely coupled with source code, teams encounter "it works on my machine" syndrome. To mitigate this, embedding environment specification generation directly into the CI/CD pipeline is invaluable. For example, regenerating and testing conda environment YAML files with each commit ensures dependencies remain synchronized and that environment drift is detected early. Moreover, whenever feasible, containerized runs should leverage pinned base images and immutable tags rather than floating `latest` tags. This guarantees deterministic environments, which is indispensable when debugging or auditing results months after initial execution.

Experiment tracking itself exposes subtle issues related to data and model artifact management. Large-scale datasets or binary models stored inefficiently within MLflow can lead to bloat and latency. One solution is to decouple heavyweight artifacts from tracking storage by integrating external artifact repositories such as cloud object stores or on-premises artifact servers. By configuring MLflow's artifact URI to external durable storage, teams maintain versioned pointers rather than redundant copies. Best practice also dictates that experiments record provenance information: dataset checksums, preprocessing scripts, and feature extraction details must all be logged systematically. This enforces end-to-end traceability and drastically reduces the time spent diagnosing performance deviations or regenerating models.

Experiment lifecycle management in MLflow benefits greatly from automated validation and quality gating mechanisms. Since MLflow does not natively enforce model evaluation criteria, teams must embed quality gates as part of their workflows. For example, integrating pre-commit hooks or pipeline stages that compare new run metrics against baseline thresholds ensures that only models exceeding performance and fairness standards progress to production. Such gates prevent the uncontrolled proliferation of poorly performing models and stimulate data scientists to maintain rigorous standards. Likewise, periodic auditing of runs tagged "production ready" can uncover hidden biases or technical debt.

Another essential practice is continuous monitoring of MLflow server and storage components. Performance bottlenecks due to log volume, concurrent run load, or metadata queries can impact productivity. Proactive monitoring via application metrics and alerting enables timely capacity scaling or archival policies. Archival of stale runs and artifacts onto cost-effective cold storage not only reduces system load but complies with data governance mandates without sacrificing accessibility. Regular backups of metadata databases and artifact storage are integral to disaster recovery strategies.

Finally, cultural factors in team adoption of MLflow often determine project success. Transparent sharing of experiment results, regular knowledge-sharing sessions, and establishment of dedicated roles such as MLflow steward or platform engineer promote best practices and tool adoption. By demystifying MLflow's tracking interface and demonstrating its value through reproducible experiments and streamlined deployment pipelines, teams foster trust and engagement. Training materials tailored to varying expertise levels also alleviate onboarding friction.

Overcoming common pitfalls in MLflow projects requires combined attention to procedural discipline, technical automation, and cultural engagement. Enforcing coherent naming and tagging conventions, maintaining strict environment control, decoupling artifact storage, embedding evaluation gates, monitoring infrastructure health, and cultivating organizational buy-in compose a robust framework. These best practices empower teams to harness MLflow's capabilities effectively, ensuring scalable, reproducible, and collaborative machine learning workflows applicable across sectors and maturity levels.

Chapter 10

Future Directions and Advanced Integrations

Peer into the horizon of machine learning operations as this chapter unveils the next generation of MLflow capabilities and its ever-expanding ecosystem. From managing generative AI models to enabling federated learning and embracing open standards, discover how practitioners and innovators are shaping MLflow's evolution to power collaborative, scalable, and future-proof AI workflows.

10.1. MLflow and Generative AI Workflows

The rapid evolution of large language models (LLMs) and generative AI has introduced unprecedented complexity in machine learning workflows, demanding extensions and adaptations of existing platforms like MLflow. Traditionally designed to manage typical supervised learning pipelines, MLflow's capabilities are increasingly being expanded to accommodate the intricacies of generative models and prompt engineering at scale. This section explores how MLflow supports these emerging requirements, focusing on robust management, evaluation, and versioning of generative AI assets.

Generative AI workflows differ from conventional models due to unique asset types: model checkpoints often reach hundreds of gigabytes, prompt templates and configurations evolve dynamically, and evaluation involves subjective, often human-in-the-loop metrics. MLflow's architecture, centered around experiment tracking, model registry, and deployment, naturally provides a foundation; however, enhancements are essential to meet generative AI needs.

Tracking Large-Scale Model Artifacts and Metadata

Handling large LLMs within MLflow begins with effective artifact management. The native MLflow artifact repository system is designed to store model binaries and related files efficiently. However, given the size of LLM checkpoints (sometimes exceeding 100 GB), integrating scalable, distributed storage backends such as Amazon S3, Azure Blob Storage, or Google Cloud Storage is essential. MLflow's ability to configure remote artifact repositories enables seamless storage of massive models, removing bottlenecks caused by local disk space.

Moreover, generative AI workflows rely heavily on diverse metadata beyond typical hyperparameters. These include:

- **Prompt Templates and Engineering Metadata**: Variants of prompt designs, their heuristics, and tuning parameters.

- **Tokenization and Embedding Configurations**: Details on vocabulary versions, tokenizer algorithms, and embedding transformations.

- **Data Provenance and Augmentation Techniques**: Descriptions of text corpora versions, synthetic data generation parameters, and pretraining corpora statistics.

MLflow's flexible `log_param` and `log_dict` methods can be leveraged to store structured JSON or YAML representations of this metadata, ensuring generation-relevant details are versioned alongside models. This is critical for reproducing outputs and understanding model behavior in generative scenarios.

Versioning Generative Models and Prompt Assets

The Model Registry component extends beyond traditional model binary versioning by incorporating process-level artifacts and intermediate results critical in generative AI. Large models often undergo multiple fine-tuning stages with different domain datasets or prompt tuning strategies. MLflow's model lineage tracking captures these iterative evolutions along with their associated evaluation metrics.

Prompt versions, a distinct asset class, require explicit versioning due to their impact on output distribution. Custom MLflow flavors can be defined to register prompt engineering files as first-class artifacts, complete with tags indicating prompt type, targeted tasks (e.g., summarization vs. question answering), and performance metrics.

An example of registering a prompt package is:

```
import mlflow

prompt_artifact_path = "prompts/v1.2/template.yaml"
with mlflow.start_run() as run:
    mlflow.log_artifact(prompt_artifact_path, artifact_path="
    prompt_templates")
    mlflow.set_tag("prompt_type", "zero-shot")
    mlflow.set_tag("target_task", "text_generation")
    mlflow.log_metric("prompt_efficiency", 0.85)
```

This treatment allows retrieval, comparison, and rollback of prompt versions akin to model checkpoints, supporting rigorous workflow reproducibility.

Evaluation and Metrics for Generative Outputs

Generative AI output evaluation transcends classical accuracy or loss metrics, requiring diverse and often qualitative assessment methods. MLflow's metric logging system accommodates scalar metrics such as BLEU, ROUGE, perplexity, and recently developed evaluation scores for text coherence and factual correctness.

For complex evaluation pipelines involving human judgments or multi-stage scoring, MLflow's experiment tracking enables structured storage of composite scores and annotator metadata. Storing evaluation artifacts such as generated text samples, annotator comments, and confusion matrices within the artifact repository facilitates detailed post hoc analysis.

Integrating automated evaluation tools within MLflow runs can be orchestrated via custom callbacks or API integrations, enabling continuous monitoring of model quality as new prompt variants or fine-tuned weights are tested.

Operationalizing Generative Models with MLflow

Deployment of large generative models mandates integration with optimized serving frameworks capable of low-latency inference at scale. MLflow's model deployment APIs support packaging and deploying these models in containerized microservices, often leveraging hardware accelerators like GPUs or TPUs.

To accommodate the dynamic nature of prompt-based inference, version-aware serving endpoints can be configured, where both the model version and corresponding prompt template version are bound together. This ensures consistency between the generation logic and the language model itself. The MLflow model registry's stage transition annotations (e.g., Staging, Production) provide governance for deployment states.

Moreover, metadata tags can enable A/B testing configurations to compare prompt-engineering strategies and fine-tuning variants systematically during deployment, facilitating continuous improvement cycles.

Best Practices for Managing Generative AI Workflows at Scale

To maximize MLflow's utility in generative AI, several best practices emerge:

- **Unified Metadata Standardization**: Define schema standards for prompt configurations, tokenization metadata, and evaluation metrics to ensure cross-collaboration consistency.

- **Automated Version Linking**: Employ scripts or pipeline integrations that automatically link related assets-models, prompts, datasets-within MLflow runs and transitions.

- **Scalable Artifacts and Storage Management**: Leverage cloud object stores with lifecycle policies (e.g., archival) to accommodate large model sizes without escalating costs.

- **Rich Experiment Tagging**: Use descriptive tags to encode contextual information, such as domain specificity, training regimes, or inference task characteristics.

- **Human-in-the-Loop Integrations**: Incorporate evaluation feedback loops within MLflow runs to improve prompt tuning and model fine-tuning iteratively.

These practices enforce traceability and accountability and enhance collaboration between data scientists, prompt engineers, and deployment teams.

Extending MLflow with Custom Plugins for Generative AI

Addressing the unique needs of generative AI in MLflow often involves extending the platform through custom plugins or experiment plugins. For example, integrating prompt management libraries or external evaluation frameworks with MLflow APIs provides a seamless interface for generative-specific operations.

A custom MLflow flavor can be developed to serialize prompt templates and associated hyperparameters in a manner directly consumable by serving frameworks. Similarly, adapter modules may be implemented within MLflow pipelines to orchestrate multimodal generative models, which combine text with images or code generation tasks.

By leveraging MLflow's extensibility, organizations can construct a tailored ecosystem that supports evolving generative AI research, experimentation, and production deployment.

MLflow's foundational capabilities are being pragmatically expanded to meet the distinctive demands of large language models and generative AI workflows. Through scalable artifact handling, detailed metadata tracking, comprehensive evaluation logging, and rigorous versioning of both models and prompts, MLflow facilitates robust lifecycle management. Adoption of best practices and custom extensions further empowers engineering teams to manage generative AI assets effectively, enabling reproducible experimentation and reliable deployment at scale.

10.2. Federated, Multi-tenant, and Cross-cloud Scenarios

Federated, multi-tenant, and cross-cloud architectures for machine learning (ML) experimentation address the increasing demand for collaborative innovation across organizational boundaries, diverse geographic locations, and heterogeneous cloud environments. These architectural paradigms extend the experimental fabric beyond single infrastructures, enabling stakeholders to pool resources, share insights, and jointly refine models while preserving data sovereignty, privacy, and operational autonomy.

At the core of federated ML experimentation is the *federated learning* paradigm, which decentralizes model training by enabling multiple participants to collaboratively train a shared model without centralizing raw data. Architecturally, this involves orchestrating iterative rounds of local model updates on participant-side data stores, followed by aggregation of these updates at a central or hierarchical server component. The aggregation step typically employs secure protocols such as secure multiparty computation or homomorphic encryption to ensure that participant contributions remain confidential. Operationally, federated pipelines must synchronize heterogeneous compute resources and handle variable bandwidths, intermittent connectivity, and local hardware constraints across regions. The scheme inherently mitigates data leakage risks by limiting data transfer, thereby conforming to strict regulatory frameworks such as GDPR or HIPAA.

Multi-tenant ML experimentation platforms extend the challenge by accommodating multiple independent organizations or teams within a shared infrastructure. This necessitates robust *isolation mechanisms* at various layers: logical isolation of datasets and model artifacts, namespace separation for experiment executions, and strict access control policies enforced via identity and access management (IAM) systems. Containerization and virtualized environments enable the dynamic provisioning of isolated sandboxes that can host experiments securely and efficiently. From an architectural standpoint, tenancy-aware orchestration engines must schedule and scale workloads to meet the diverse and concurrent demands of several tenants. The design also involves fine-grained resource quotas, fair scheduling policies, and monitoring telemetry to maintain service-level objectives (SLOs) across tenants. On the privacy front, tenants require guarantees that their data, intermediate model states, and hyperparameters are inaccessible to other participants, which can be addressed through encryption, differential privacy techniques, and audit trails.

Cross-cloud ML experimentation introduces complexity stemming from heterogeneity in cloud service provider offerings, networking models, and operational interfaces. Architectures enabling cross-cloud workflows often leverage *cloud-agnostic abstraction layers* or orchestration middleware capable of deploying and managing ML experiments seamlessly across multiple cloud environments. For example, Kubernetes-based platforms with federated cluster management provide common APIs and reproducible environments that mask provider-specific nuances. Data synchronization across clouds is optimized through selective data placement strategies, caching, and incremental delta transfers, reducing latency and cost. Security considerations become paramount, requiring end-to-end encryption of data in transit and at rest, federated identity solutions for unified authentication, and the consistent application of security policies across clouds. Additionally, compliance regimes must be reconciled with data residency requirements and industry-specific certifications, posing governance challenges. Cross-cloud experimentation facilitates leveraging specialized hardware accelerators and cost arbitrage but mandates intricate billing, cost allocation, and usage accounting models.

In all scenarios, interoperability and standardization are critical enablers. Protocols such as the Open Neural Network Exchange (ONNX) provide a common format for model exchange, promoting portability and reuse of ML artifacts between disparate systems. Metadata standards, experiment tracking frameworks, and API consistency allow reproducible and traceable experimentation across collaborative environments.

A representative workflow in these distributed experimentations involves the following stages:

- Local data preprocessing and feature extraction;
- Initialization of a shared model reference;
- Local training or fine-tuning per participant or tenant;
- Transmission of encrypted model updates to a central or federated aggregator;

- Aggregation applying secure computation primitives; and

- Dissemination of the updated global model back to participants.

Orchestration systems must provide fault tolerance, detecting and compensating for straggler nodes, partial failures, or data drift. Transparent and auditable logging of experiment steps, parameter versions, and dataset schemas ensures trust and accountability.

The principal challenges confronting federated, multi-tenant, and cross-cloud experimentation include managing heterogeneous environments, enforcing consistent security models, optimizing communication overheads, and maintaining scalability amidst growing numbers of collaborators. Furthermore, latency constraints and data heterogeneity can impair convergence rates and generalization of models. Advanced research into adaptive aggregation algorithms, privacy-preserving protocols, and cross-domain transfer learning is actively addressing these issues.

Together, these architectural and operational solutions empower organizations to embrace collaborative ML experimentation models that transcend institutional and geographic boundaries. Such capabilities accelerate innovation cycles, improve model robustness by incorporating diverse data sources, and comply with stringent privacy and regulatory mandates-thus defining the future frontier of distributed machine learning experimentation.

10.3. Collaborative, Distributed Experimentation

The evolution of machine learning (ML) workflows towards collaborative, distributed experimentation marks a critical advance in MLOps practices. This progression transcends the siloed development paradigms of earlier stages, enabling cross-geographical and cross-disciplinary teams to co-develop models, share lineage information, and exert dynamic governance over ML assets. The integration of emerging features and standardized patterns in tooling and infrastructure has facilitated this transformation, improving scalability, reproducibility, and innovation velocity across organizations.

At the core of collaborative distributed experimentation lies the concept of *shared lineage*, a paradigm whereby the provenance and evolution of datasets, feature transformations, model versions, and evaluation metrics are transparently tracked and accessible to all stakeholders. Shared lineage systems capture the full topology of artifact dependencies and transformations, enabling rigorous traceability and impact analysis. These systems often rely on directed acyclic graph (DAG) representations of workflows, where each node represents an artifact or computation step, and directed edges signify data flow or dependency. Centralized or federated metadata stores underpin this graph, ensuring consistency and discoverability while respecting organizational access controls.

Dynamic governance mechanisms extend this concept by embedding policy enforcement and access control directly into the lineage-aware infrastructure. Policies can define permissible experiments, data usage constraints, or model promotion criteria, and be evaluated automatically during pipeline execution or artifact registration. This incorporation of governance into the experimentation lifecycle mitigates risks associated with unauthorized data access, compliance violations, and model drift while preserving agility. Tools supporting fine-grained role-based and attribute-based access controls, coupled with immutable audit trails, constitute essential components of governance frameworks.

The co-development aspect leverages version control principles and collaborative workflows tailored for ML assets. Unlike traditional source code, ML artifacts include large datasets, serialized models, and complex pipeline configurations, necessitating specialized storage and diffing mechanisms. Data version control systems (e.g., DVC, MLflow) facilitate branching, merging, and synchronization of such assets alongside code, ensuring experiments can be iterated and shared with precision. These systems are often augmented by APIs that enable automated synchronization with continuous integration/continuous deployment (CI/CD) pipelines and experiment tracking platforms, providing seamless integration of collaboration into automated workflows.

APIs play a pivotal role in connecting diverse tooling, enabling interoperability across heterogeneous environments. Emerging standards such as the Open Metadata Initiative (OMI) and ML Schema facilitate consistent schema definitions and operations across platforms, easing data interchange and lineage capture. Furthermore, API-first designs empower programmatic control over workspace creation, experiment orchestration, and model deployment, enabling dynamic resource allocation and on-demand sharing of experimental runs. These interfaces support federated experimentation environments where distributed teams can contribute asynchronously yet maintain a consistent global state of experimentation artifacts.

Collaboration tools, including integrated notebooks, annotation interfaces, and issue tracking systems, are increasingly integrated within distributed experimentation ecosystems. Real-time co-editing capabilities and commenting enhance synchronous collaboration, while asynchronous communication is supported through artifact-centric discussion threads. Separation of concerns is maintained via workspace isolation and permissions, enabling multiple teams to work on shared projects without conflict. Visualization dashboards aggregate metrics and lineage data, providing holistic situational awareness to engineers, data scientists, and stakeholders alike.

Patterns of distributed experimentation often incorporate *param-*

eter search at scale across cloud or hybrid environments. Job orchestration systems schedule experiments efficiently while respecting resource quotas and equipoise between fairness and experimentation speed. Results are automatically aggregated and compared through shared tracking repositories. Model registries linked with lineage systems expedite model governance by supporting version locking, staged rollouts, and deprecation workflows collaboratively managed by cross-functional teams.

The impact of these advancements is reflected in several metrics: reduced experimental turnaround time by enabling parallelism and reuse; improved reproducibility through comprehensive lineage and versioning; and elevated model quality via collaborative review and governance. Moreover, organizations benefit from minimized knowledge loss as context and rationale behind experimental decisions are preserved within artifact metadata, rather than siloed in disparate communication channels. This preservation fosters knowledge transfer and accelerates onboarding for new members of distributed teams.

Collaborative, distributed experimentation represents an orchestration of lineage-aware infrastructure, dynamic governance, comprehensive version control, and API-driven interoperability. Together, these components empower distributed teams to co-develop ML assets with traceability, transparency, and compliance. The consequent enhancement in productivity and robustness of ML pipelines lays the groundwork for scalable MLOps practices that continuously harness collective expertise across organizational boundaries.

10.4. Custom Plugins and MLflow Extensions

The extensibility of MLflow is a key factor in its widespread adoption, particularly in complex environments where default components require customization to fit specialized workflows or enterprise ecosystems. This section focuses on the architectural pathways and community resources that facilitate the development, distribution, and integration of custom MLflow plugins. These plugins extend MLflow's core functionalities, enabling organizations to tailor experiment tracking, model deployment, and metadata management to their unique requirements.

MLflow's plugin mechanism primarily hinges on its modular design and clearly defined API surfaces, which provide stable extension points. Plugins in MLflow are typically conceived as Python packages that expose specific entry points conforming to the MLflow plugin interface. These entry points allow the augmentation or complete replacement of core MLflow behaviors without modifying the codebase of the MLflow platform itself. The following key components highlight the extensibility paradigm:

- **Plugin API surfaces**: MLflow exposes abstract base classes and method signatures that plugins must implement. For example, the `mlflow.projects` module allows custom project runners, and the `mlflow.pyfunc` interface supports custom Python model flavors. Plugin developers leverage these predefined contracts to ensure compatibility and integration fidelity.

- **Extension hooks**: MLflow provides well-defined hooks, such as the model "flavor" system, where users can register new flavors representing different model types or serialization formats. These hooks enable runtime discovery and invocation of extended functionalities during model logging, loading, and serving.

- **Discovery and registration**: Plugins are discoverable via Python package metadata, specifically using entry points defined in the `setup.py` or `pyproject.toml` files. MLflow scans these entry points at startup, dynamically loading and registering plugins without requiring manual configuration within the MLflow environment.

To illustrate the creation of an MLflow plugin, consider a scenario where a custom model flavor is required to support a proprietary machine learning framework. The development proceeds by defining a new flavor with corresponding serialization, deserialization, and prediction logic. The plugin package structure conforms to Python standards and declares an entry point as follows in setup.py:

```
setup(
    name="mlflow-proprietary-flavor",
    version="0.1.0",
    packages=find_packages(),
    entry_points={
        "mlflow.pyfunc": [
            "proprietary_flavor = mlflow_proprietary_flavor:
        ProprietaryFlavor"
        ],
    },
)
```

Within the mlflow_proprietary_flavor module, the class ProprietaryFlavor implements methods such as save_model(), load_model(), and predict() matching MLflow's pyfunc flavor API. Integrating the plugin enables transparent usage with MLflow commands such as mlflow.pyfunc.log_model or mlflow.pyfunc.load_model, effectively bridging MLflow's ecosystem with the custom framework.

Community engagement plays a vital role in harnessing the power of custom plugins. MLflow's open-source ecosystem hosts a range of widely adopted extensions, from specialized model flavors supporting frameworks like XGBoost and TensorFlow Extended (TFX), to alternative artifact stores and authentication mechanisms. Developers are encouraged to explore the official MLflow GitHub repository's plugin directory and the accompanying discussion forums where design patterns, best practices, and maintenance strategies are actively shared. This ecosystem fosters innovation by enabling users to iterate rapidly on prototypes and evolve them into robust, production-grade plugins.

From prototype to production, the evolution of MLflow plugins necessitates adherence to several critical considerations:

- **API stability and compatibility**: MLflow strives to maintain backwards compatibility within stable API versions. Plugin developers must monitor MLflow's changelogs and test compatibility to avoid regressions during upgrades.

- **Testing and validation**: Comprehensive unit and integration testing ensures that plugins behave consistently across different MLflow versions and deployment environments. It is advisable to use continuous integration pipelines compatible with MLflow's testing strategy.

- **Documentation and distribution**: Effective documentation enhances usability and adoption. Packaging plugins for distribution on PyPI or internal artifact repositories facilitates installation and version management.

- **Security and compliance**: Plugins interacting with sensitive data or deploying models to production environments should conform to organizational security policies, including code audits and runtime sandboxing if appropriate.

In terms of runtime integration, MLflow also supports extending the REST API and UI layers through custom plugins, although these aspects require deeper familiarity with MLflow's internal server structure and React.js frontend. Advanced users can provide backend server plugins that introduce new REST endpoints or modify existing behaviors, as well as frontend plugins that enhance the UI with new panels or visualizations. These extensions contribute to tailored user experiences particularly suited to enterprise data science teams and MLOps pipelines.

An MLflow custom plugin typically progresses through the following phases:

1. **Design**: Define the extension scope, API surface implementation, and integration points.

2. **Prototype**: Implement minimum viable functionality to validate operational concepts.

3. **Package**: Structure the code as a Python package with appropriate metadata and entry points.

4. **Test**: Develop unit, integration, and system tests covering MLflow version compatibility.

5. **Distribute**: Publish to package repositories or internal distribution channels.

6. **Operate**: Integrate into MLflow deployments, monitor performance, and gather user feedback for iterative improvements.

MLflow's plugin framework deliberately balances flexibility with stability, empowering developers to innovate while mitigating fragmentation risks. By mastering these mechanisms and leveraging community resources, data science and MLOps practitioners can significantly enhance MLflow's adaptability, driving better reproducibility, scalability, and automation in modern machine learning workflows.

10.5. Open Standards and Interoperability

The rapid expansion of machine learning (ML) applications across diverse industries has intensified the demand for frameworks and tools that enable flexible, scalable, and maintainable workflows. Within this context, MLflow emerges as a pivotal orchestration layer that facilitates experimentation, reproducibility, and deployment of ML models. A crucial aspect of MLflow's appeal lies in its support for open standards and interoperability, providing a mechanism to future-proof ML workflows and bridge heterogeneous environments efficiently.

Central to achieving interoperability in ML workflows is the adoption of open and standardized formats. The Open Neural Network Exchange (ONNX) format, for example, has become a principal vehicle for model portability. ONNX enables the representation of models in a framework-agnostic manner, permitting models trained in one environment to be deployed or further refined in another. MLflow's integration with ONNX allows practitioners to log and manage ONNX models within its tracking and registry components seamlessly. This integration not only facilitates a unified model lifecycle management experience but also abstracts away complexities inherent in transitioning models across platforms.

The capability to save models in ONNX format through MLflow entails export functions that convert models trained with diverse ML libraries such as PyTorch, TensorFlow, or Scikit-learn into the standardized ONNX graph format. By leveraging MLflow's `mlflow.onnx` API, users can log ONNX artifacts during experiments, enabling reproducible deployment pipelines that are agnostic to underlying frameworks. This interoperability ensures that downstream services can consume models without dependence on the original training environment, mitigating vendor lock-in and fostering collaboration across teams with heterogeneous tool preferences.

Beyond ONNX, emerging efforts such as MLSpec aim to establish comprehensive specifications for ML artifacts, spanning dataset formats, model metadata, evaluation protocols, and deployment specifications. Although MLSpec remains an evolving initiative, it complements ONNX by addressing dimensions of ML workflows not fully covered by model exchange formats alone. MLflow's modular architecture and extensibility framework position it well to incorporate such open specification standards as they mature, enhancing the expressiveness and portability of experiment data, versioning, and audit trails alongside models themselves.

Embracing open standards through MLflow confers several strategic advantages. First, it future-proofs workflows by decoupling model serialization and deployment from proprietary frameworks or runtime environments. As the ML landscape constantly evolves, new frameworks and hardware accelerators emerge, making adherence to open formats a safeguard against obsolescence. Second, it simplifies integration within diverse ecosystem components, such as feature stores, data versioning systems, and model deployment platforms, by providing a shared contractual interface for models and their metadata.

Interoperability also plays a critical role in enabling reproducibility and collaborative development. Teams distributed across different geographical locations and using disparate tools can standardize on MLflow's open format capabilities as a lingua franca for exchanging machine learning assets. Through MLflow's model registry and tracking server, models adhering to open standards like ONNX can be cataloged with rich metadata, facilitating governance and audit compliance in regulated domains.

Furthermore, MLflow's support for open models extends naturally into deployment scenarios such as containerization and serverless function hosting. By packaging models in standard formats, MLflow enables consistent environment reproducibility and seamless dependency management. This approach aligns well with continuous integration and continuous delivery (CI/CD) pipelines, allowing automated validation, canary testing, and rollback of ML models with minimal friction.

Another dimension of interoperability is present in MLflow's integration with cloud services and ML platforms that inherently support open standards. For instance, many managed services consume ONNX models for accelerated inference on specialized hardware (e.g., GPUs and TPUs). MLflow's capability to export and register models in ONNX format thus facilitates direct deployment into these infrastructure offerings. The resulting portability reduces overhead and complexity for data science teams transitioning from experimentation to production.

In summary, MLflow's embracement of open standards such as ONNX and its alignment with emerging specifications like ML-Spec underpin a strategy to foster interoperability, scalability, and lifecycle consistency. This approach mitigates risks associated with proprietary lock-in and technology fragmentation, providing a resilient foundation for evolving ML ecosystems. By integrating diverse tooling and frameworks through standardized formats, MLflow acts as a unifying substrate that streamlines the operationalization of machine learning at scale.

```python
import mlflow
import mlflow.onnx
import onnx
from skl2onnx import convert_sklearn
from skl2onnx.common.data_types import FloatTensorType
from sklearn.datasets import load_iris
from sklearn.linear_model import LogisticRegression

# Train a simple sklearn model
data = load_iris()
X, y = data.data, data.target
model = LogisticRegression(max_iter=1000)
model.fit(X, y)

# Convert sklearn model to ONNX
initial_type = [('float_input', FloatTensorType([None, X.shape
    [1]]))]
onnx_model = convert_sklearn(model, initial_types=initial_type)

# Log ONNX model with MLflow
with mlflow.start_run():
    mlflow.onnx.log_model(onnx_model, "model",
        registered_model_name="Iris_ONNX_Model")
```

```
Registered model 'Iris_ONNX_Model' version 1 created successfully.
Model logged to run with ID '...'
```

255

10.6.   The Next Decade of MLflow and MLOps

The evolution of MLflow within the next decade will be inseparable from the broader progression of MLOps, driven by advancements in research, maturation of community practices, and the expanding scope of machine learning deployment. MLflow, as a widely adopted open-source platform for managing the machine learning lifecycle, provides an instructive lens through which to anticipate the future of MLOps at large.

One of the foremost trends shaping MLflow's trajectory is the increasing emphasis on end-to-end automation and abstraction in the MLOps pipeline. Current MLflow components—tracking, projects, models, and model registry—provide modular capabilities that users must integrate with external orchestration and deployment tools. The next decade will likely see MLflow evolving into a more cohesive and automated ecosystem, possibly incorporating native orchestration and real-time governance capabilities. Advances in declarative MLOps specifications and workflow descriptions will drive this integration, enabling users to define complex machine learning pipelines that adapt dynamically to changing data conditions and model feedback loops without extensive custom engineering.

Active research in automated machine learning (AutoML) and continuous learning paradigms will increasingly influence MLflow's capabilities. AutoML pipelines, which optimize hyperparameters, architectures, and even feature engineering automatically, necessitate tight coupling between experiment tracking and optimized resource management. MLflow may expand its native support to encompass meta-learning approaches that facilitate transfer across related tasks, drastically reducing training latency and improving model efficiency. Furthermore, the proliferation of models that learn continuously from streaming or evolving datasets will require MLflow and similar platforms to adopt incremental versioning schemes and fine-grained artifact tracking beyond static snapshots. This evolution will enable enhanced reproducibility and auditability for models that adjust after initial deployment.

Community-driven innovation will remain a cornerstone of MLflow's growth, particularly through the diversification of its plugin architecture and contributions from major cloud and edge providers. As ML workloads shift increasingly toward distributed, federated, and edge environments, MLflow will need to natively support heterogeneous infrastructures with varying compute, storage, and privacy constraints. The integration of secure multiparty computation and differential privacy into model training and deployment workflows will be crucial for industries handling sensitive data. The community's ability to collaboratively develop and share such privacy-preserving extensions will dictate MLflow's adoption in regulated sectors like healthcare and finance.

The broader MLOps landscape will also be shaped by advancing standards and interoperability protocols. The success of MLflow's model packaging formats may inspire more universal standards for ML metadata, enabling seamless migration of models and pipelines across platforms. This standardization effort, already nascent through initiatives like the Open Neural Network Exchange (ONNX) and the ML Metadata schema, will culminate in a more federated MLOps ecosystem where models can be audited, updated, and monitored transparently regardless of underlying tooling. Such openness will facilitate robust compliance with evolving regulations and strengthen trustworthiness in AI systems.

Another anticipated innovation pertains to explainability and AI ethics baked into MLOps pipelines. MLflow may extend its tracking and registry features to encompass explainability artifacts generated during experimentation and deployment. Future MLOps platforms will not only maintain model versions but also document interpretability metrics, fairness assessments, provenance of training data, and human-in-the-loop feedback. This richer metadata ecosystem will promote the deployment of more accountable and transparent ML systems by default, aligning development workflows with broader societal values and regulatory expectations.

Moreover, as machine learning advances into more complex modalities such as large-scale generative models and reinforcement learning-driven autonomous systems, MLflow and MLOps workflows will adapt to accommodate diverse artifact types and lifecycle dynamics. For instance, handling model ensembles with billions of parameters or lifelong learning agents operating in non-stationary environments demands novel registries and deployment abstractions that go beyond traditional model checkpoints. This will likely lead to the emergence of hierarchical or graph-based model management systems, where versions are linked not only temporally but also by functional dependencies and collaborative relationships.

The next decade will witness MLflow transforming from a foundational experiment and model management platform into an integrated, intelligent, and privacy-aware MLOps ecosystem. This transformation will be driven by convergence of automated machine learning, continual learning, robust privacy mechanisms, open standards, and ethical AI considerations. The sustained engagement of a vibrant global community coupled with interdisciplinary research will shape tools that enable organizations to deliver machine learning projects with unprecedented speed, robustness, and accountability. As machine learning penetrates ever more sectors and applications, MLflow's evolution will illuminate the principles and practices essential for scalable, transparent, and trustworthy AI deployment in the years ahead.

www.ingramcontent.com/pod-product-compliance
Lightning Source LLC
Chambersburg PA
CBHW061241220326
41599CB00028B/5497